With best wishes from
Claire Macdonald of Macdonald

CLAIRE MACDONALD'S
SCOTLAND

THE BEST OF SCOTTISH FOOD AND DRINK

CLAIRE MACDONALD'S
SCOTLAND

THE BEST OF SCOTTISH FOOD AND DRINK

WITH PHOTOGRAPHS BY JOHN FERRO SIMS

A BULFINCH PRESS BOOK
LITTLE, BROWN AND COMPANY
BOSTON TORONTO LONDON

Some Useful Notes

In the recipes, measures are given in the following order:
Imperial/American cups and spoons (where required)/Metric.
All three measures have been calculated separately,
and they are not exact equivalents. Therefore, when preparing
a recipe, use just one set of measures.
All spoon measures are level and are based on the following
metric equivalents:
1 teaspoon = 5 ml   1 tablespoon = 15 ml
These correspond very closely to standard American spoon measures.
However, Australian readers should note that their tablespoon
contains 20 ml.
American equivalents for ingredients and terminology are given in
parentheses in the recipes.
Where sugar is called for in a recipe, use granulated unless
otherwise specified.
Cooking times may vary slightly depending on individual ovens,
so use the timings in the recipes only as a guide.

Text copyright © 1990 by Claire Macdonald
Photographs copyright © 1990 by John Ferro Sims

First Edition

A C I P catalogue record for this book
is available from the British Library.

Library of Congress Cataloging-in-Publication Data

Macdonald of Macdonald, Lady.
Lady Macdonald's Scotland: the best of Scottish food and drink/Lady
Macdonald. — 1st ed.
p.   cm.
ISBN 0-8212-1809-3
1. Cookery, Scottish. 2. Beverages — Scotland. I. Title.
TX717.3.M3 1990   90-1747
641.59411 — dc20

Designed by Andrew Barron and Collis Clements Associates
Typeset by Wyvern Typesetting Ltd, Bristol

Published simultaneously in the United States of
America by Bulfinch Press, an imprint and
trademark of Little, Brown and Company (Inc.),
in Great Britain by Little, Brown and Company (UK) Ltd,
and in Canada by Little, Brown & Company (Canada) Limited

PRINTED IN GERMANY

*Photograph on page 1: Evening light across
Glenurquhart, near Inverness. Pages 2/3
sunset at Loch Eil from Inverlochy Castle.*

Contents

FOREWORD

Scotland used not to be noted for its cooking, but in
the last decade or so it has produced some of the
best chefs in Europe. It has also produced a number
of small hotels where the food and welcome are
equal to any found overseas, and which strive to
provide the best for their guests. In this book I shall
be writing about some of the places where you can
stay in comfort and sample the best cooking.
It is a very personal view of my adopted country.

I FEEL it is a great responsibility to be in a position to welcome people into our home at Kinloch (which is a small hotel) as well as to write about food in Scotland. The Scots have the best in the world when it comes to beef, lamb and pork, game, fish and shellfish, soft fruits and, ever increasingly, cheeses. And they are renowned the world over for their baking skills; not the fine patisserie of France and Italy, but a more homely and comforting sort of baking, incorporating scones and pancakes, and sustaining fruit cakes and shortbread.

The Scots, over the centuries, have perfected the art of preservation by smoking, and smoked salmon has for years been considered one of the greatest delicacies (although, personally, I would as soon eat a really good kipper).

I have specifically been given the difficult task of choosing my ten favourite hotels for this book. There are easily another ten which I would include, given the space. One of the very good things about being in this way of life (it could hardly be described as a job) is the friendship that exists between us – well, most of us, certainly all of us in this book, as well as a good few more. People outside our business imagine that we are all deadly rivals – they couldn't be more wrong.

Above: The entrance to Pittodrie House, Aberdeenshire.
Opposite top: An alder in the autumn mist along
the River Spey. Bottom: The evening sky, Raasay.

In the months when we are closed we all like to get together at some point, and we genuinely enjoy each other's company. When we are open, hardly a week goes by without telephone calls between us, usually to see if there is any available accommodation for guests who want to visit another area.

Readers of this book will notice a definite west-coast bias among the hotels. That is because a great many guests plan their Scottish holidays so as to stay at Airds or Ardsheal House (they are only half an hour apart), followed by Inverlochy, then us, before going up to Altnaharrie.

In fact, so many do this that I often think that some people might be under the illusion that we provide some sort of up-market package holiday. This is not the case! But it accounts for the fact that we all belong in this book, as do Polmaily, at Drumnadrochit, with whom we often exchange guests, as well as the Dower House, on the Black Isle north of Inverness. Pittodrie, near Aberdeen, is a beautiful spot and yet so close (only half an hour's drive) to Aberdeen. And the Peat Inn is one of the best restaurants in Great Britain, let alone Scotland, and also has lovely bedroom suites. Cringletie makes an excellent place to stay and enjoy really good food, as well as the hospitality of the owners, in the heart of the Border country. All the hotels are owner occupied and run.

Other hotels which are not in this book, but which I would like to mention, include the Kinlochbervie Hotel, the Summer Isles Hotel and Tullich Lodge, as well as Dunain Park Hotel. All of these fall into the right category for this book, giving comfort, extremely good food, and really personal service. Ours may not all be super de-luxe establishments – Kinloch certainly isn't – but they are houses rather than hotels, with antiques, old books and objects of interest, and are places where we like to think our guests feel at home.

We all place the emphasis on our cooking. We all take continuing trouble to get the very best produce we can, and this becomes easier as the choice widens, although there will always be logistical problems to contend with. The wider choice is made possible by the increasing numbers of enterprising people growing organic vegetables and fruit, for example: by enterprises like Scotherbs which, in the six years since it was founded, has made fresh herbs available in an abundance never seen before in Scotland; by our butchers, who really appreciate what excellent meat is raised in Scotland;

our fish merchants, who take the trouble to telephone us when they receive a special delivery in case we are interested; our game dealers, who know to keep special items for us – what all our suppliers have in common is a concern for us, and total reliability. And how we appreciate them – we couldn't give our guests the sort of food we do without such dependable suppliers.

Maintaining a hotel, especially in fairly wild and rugged countryside like this, is a constant battle – rather like painting the Forth road bridge: once you have got to the end it is time to start again. Not long ago David Wilson of the Peat Inn was ruefully pointing out to me the builders on his roof, who are replacing a large part of it – as he says, no visitor to the Peat Inn will notice the thousands of pounds he has spent on the roof! I fully sympathize, because here at Kinloch about half of our roof is being replaced even as I write! Each winter, when we close for three months, a carefully planned refurbishment scheme is carried out. In fact those three months fly by very fast, what with all that goes on in that time, including quantities of marmalade making, which I love.

The two groups of people without whom none of us could run our businesses are the guests and our staff. The vast majority of our guests are positive life-enhancers. I frequently feel really glad to be in the line of business that we are, because otherwise I just wouldn't meet such a large number of very nice people, of all nationalities. But there are the inevitable one or two each season for whom we are not the ideal. It is truly a case of not being able to please everyone all the time, but if only such people knew just how they can cast one down . . .

Floors Castle, near Kelso, is an impressive eighteenth-century mansion set in beautiful grounds.

although perhaps it would make no difference, because life does contain a very few people who take pleasure in complaining.

Our staff are our all, and we are all very lucky in having a large nucleus of permanent people. In our case life at Kinloch is not dissimilar to life in a commune, I rather suspect. Inevitably each year one, or two if we are very unlucky, of those who come to work with us find the remoteness oppressive – or that they can't stand the midges! It doesn't matter how hard I stress the extreme isolation of our setting at Kinloch, it is only by living and working here that it can be experienced at first hand. Also, work in a hotel is extremely hard – another fact which I stress – and life is composed of workers and non-workers.

There is scant regard among us for the numerous hotel guides, most of which show no interest in the sheer quality which hotels like ours have to offer. Their rating systems appear to be completely inflexible. A hotel may score highly in the dining-room, and then fall foul of some ludicrous criterion of 'excellence' which any mediocre chain hotel can satisfy automatically but which would be nonsensical in a place like ours. The A A inspectors, for example, now expect to find telephones and colour televisions in the bedrooms. (Godfrey and I do have a television, but we know that our guests don't come to Kinloch to watch it.)

Perhaps we should all resign ourselves to the fact that most guides are simply not on our wavelength and that, just as the R A C Rally will never be won by a Rolls-Royce, we will never find favour with organizations which are not in sympathy with our aims. The Scottish Tourist Board is such an organization. They award their 'crowns' without any regard for the quality of food, welcome or service. Moreover, many of us have found their inspectors arrogant to the point of rudeness. A recent coup by an S T B inspector was to penalize the Dower House for having a sofa in the dining-room!

While it is obviously galling to see the charms of hotels such as ours being overlooked on account of this blinkered attitude, it is downright infuriating to see reports which are inaccurate or unfair. The Taylors, at Ardsheal, were stung by a report in the 1990 *Good Hotel Guide* which referred to their soap as cheap – when it comes from Crabtree and Evelyn. The same guide quoted a report complaining that if you hung something

Looking across Glenurquhart from the hills above Polmaily
House Hotel, one of my "Establishments of Distinction".

on a hook in the bathroom of one of the bedrooms at Airds, you obscured the view in the mirror. Oh dear. Sadly, there will always be people who love to look for niggles, and this makes good reading, presumably, in the opinion of the editors of some of these guides.

There are honourable exceptions. Egon Ronay may not be a thrilling read but is a reliable source of information on what is provided at each establishment. Better still are two new guides, Wendy Arnold's *The Historic Hotels of Scotland* and Karen Brown's *English, Welsh and Scottish Country Inns*, which are free of prejudices and, instead of relying on reports from readers, show a concern for accuracy and a genuine interest in the places they describe.

While the Scottish Tourist Board just doesn't cater for hotels like ourselves, and Ardsheal, in their new ratings scheme, I do feel that hotels like all of us in the book are responsible for enticing a fair number of visitors to Scotland each year from overseas. If journalists from prestigious food magazines like *Gourmet*, for example, ask to come and stay to write about us, as has recently happened to Betty Allen of Airds, Gunn Eriksen of Altnaharrie, and me here at Kinloch in one article, then this can't be bad for Scotland.

There is nowhere in the world as beautiful as Scotland, especially when the weather is fine. But even the uncertainty of the weather adds somehow to the mysticism of the country. I can't think of living anywhere else – except occasionally when the midges are at their worst and I catch myself thinking longingly of Italy, but these are rare occasions!

I would like to thank several people who have been involved with this book. Firstly, to Godfrey, my husband, for his tolerance and support – and indeed his encouragement when needed – thank you darling! Secondly, a big thank you to John Ferro Sims, who took the wonderful photographs. John is the least prima donna-like (or perhaps I should say primo uomo-like) artist to work with, and everyone who met him on his travels through Scotland for this book rang me to tell me how much they had enjoyed his visit, and how painless the photography sessions were! John, thank you very much. Thanks also to Andrew Barron, for his elegant design, and to Vivien Bowler, who asked me to write this book. It is always a treat to get a chance to sing the praises of Scotland.

Claire Macdonald of Macdonald
Kinloch, January 1990

THE MACDONALDS
—— AT ——
KINLOCH LODGE

This is the hardest bit of the book to write.
Whereas one can look objectively at what other hotels
are like – observing, as it were, from the receiving end –
we can only write about Kinloch from the giving
end. How can I tell what it is like to stay at Kinloch?
All I can really do is to describe what we try to
provide for our guests who come and stay with us
here on the Isle of Skye.

Opposite: Sunset over the Cuillin hills taken from
Ord, Skye. Above: The author standing in front
of a painting of one of her husband's ancestors.

KINLOCH IS at the southern end of Skye, nearly forty miles from the island capital, Portree. My husband Godfrey's family have owned Kinloch Lodge for three hundred years. They used to live down the road in Armadale Castle until Godfrey's father was born to the second son of the 6th Baron and 20th High Chief of Clan Donald. At this point Godfrey's grandparents moved to Ostaig House and that's where he was born in 1947. After our marriage we lived there till 1982, when we built on to Kinloch, which had been run as a hotel since 1973, and made it our home. Built in 1680 Kinloch Lodge is a stark but elegant white house, at the head of Loch Na Dal (the word Kinloch means head of the loch) and at the foot of a hill, home of three herds of red deer. The Macdonald family used Kinloch as a shooting lodge, visiting the house and staying for weeks on end.

It is a beautiful setting, with the hill behind, lovely views on two sides and our wonderfully isolated position – we are a mile down a bumpy road from the 'main' road, which itself is only single track and tends to be very congested in the summer – which draw many guests to Kinloch. They come here in search of peace, looking forward to doing nothing more than walk, admire the views, and study our marvellous wildlife.

This whole area is designated one of special scientific interest, with otters and seals living in the waters round the house, and many different species of seabird, including herons and divers. Up the hill behind us we regularly see golden eagles and on walks up the forestry track we have been lucky enough to see as many as three at one time. The wild flowers and shrubs are lovely – first come the snowdrops, then, as spring progresses, huge clumps of primroses and plenty of sturdy violets appear in the woods beside us. The bluebells and wild garlic overlap with the primroses, and then come the rhododendrons for which the west coast of Scotland is famous. After the rhododendrons, there is an abundance of beautiful shrubs and flowers – we have two botanists who visit us every year in July, and from whom we have learnt a great deal about the numerous rare flora growing around us. There are several species of wild orchid, and wherever you walk around Kinloch during the summer months you smell the wonderful fragrance of bog myrtle.

The house was built long before the Victorians brought to Scotland the baronial splendour of their architecture. There is no panelling here, and neither of our two drawing-rooms is very large. The dining-room comfortably contains the ten or eleven tables for our guests, yet in the winter months, when the family use the dining-room with just one long table and the others are put away, it never looks too empty.

Downstairs the house is brightly decorated in colours I love. One drawing-room is apricot-coloured, the other is raspberry-coloured, and the dining-room is dark green. Throughout the rooms and corridors there are family portraits, photographs, books, ornaments and vases of flowers. The dining-room is full of silver, and at dinner the polished wood tables are set with silver and crystal. At breakfast time we have tablecloths on the tables, and guests help themselves from the sideboard.

Upstairs we have ten bedrooms, three of which are of a comfortable size, the remainder distinctly on the small side. They are all prettily wallpapered and curtained, with comfy beds, books, ornaments and pictures. They are all equipped with electric blankets and hair-dryers, but none of our rooms has a telephone or television – nor will they have, because this is a country house and I feel strongly that a phone in the room tempts guests to spend time talking to business colleagues, when I feel that really they are here to unwind and get away from all that. This is not an original thought of mine, I must confess, but once when I was wondering aloud to a journalist friend of mine

Above: One of the finest examples of the great Scottish breakfast is to be found at Kinloch. Opposite: The dining-room where breakfast and dinner are served.

Kinloch Lodge is situated at the southern end of Skye, at the head
of Loch Na Dal (the word Kinloch means head of the loch).

whether we should install a telephone system, that was his response, with which I agree whole-heartedly! As for television, well, we do have one, tucked away behind a chair in the small drawing-room, but guests hardly ever ask to watch television, unless there is an election going on, or it is finals day at Wimbledon.

When we first opened Kinloch, sixteen years ago, neither of us had any formal training in hotel management whatsoever. I had worked as a cook, but had no formal training, and, much more important, Godfrey had done five years' training as a chartered accountant in Edinburgh. But we did have a clear idea of what we wanted to provide for our guests: essentially what we ourselves would like to find in a house-like hotel in such a situation as ours. Tying for top place in our list of priorities were – and still are – good food, warmth and comfort,

within a fairly informal and relaxed atmosphere. We both love good food and wine, and the sort of food provided at Kinloch then and now can best be described as high quality dinner party food. In our first year we were lucky enough to have working with us Peter Macpherson and Millie MacLure, both of whom were living locally. Neither had any cookery training, but both had, and still have, a real flair for cooking. Between us we learned as we went along, mostly from the Cordon Bleu magazines, which had excellent colour illustrations, to show us what we were aiming for!

In our first years our great problem was supplies: we knew what we wanted to give our guests, but we just couldn't get the wherewithal. We had a fresh fruit and vegetable delivery once every two weeks, and that lorry delivered first to the shops and then to the hotels, so what

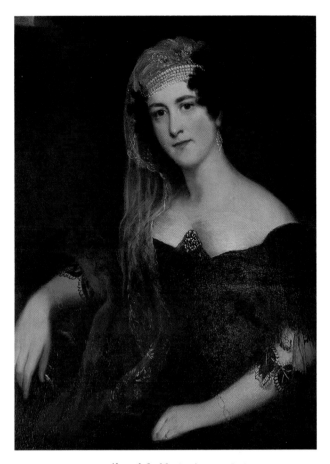

Above left: Maria Augusta Lukin-Wyndham, mother of Maria, wife of the fourth Lord Macdonald.
Right: Helen Macdonald (nee Banks), my husband Godfrey's grandmother.

they had left after two or three days was hardly worth buying anyway. We grew our own vegetables and herbs, but they were dependent on the weather, and our second year was an extremely wet one: I remember not being able to hang out the washing – which included many nappies for our eldest – more than about ten times in four months. Our supplies were dependent on trips away, to add some interest to our staple diet.

Now, thankfully, the story is very different and an altogether happier one. We have wonderful suppliers, and I shall be telling you about them in the following chapters. I'm even glad we experienced the supply diffi-culties in our early years because it means we shall *never* take for granted the excellence of our suppliers now. Our fruit and vegetables – those that we don't buy organically grown – are supplied by Norman Macleod, who is a

wholesaler and retailer based in Portree. He started a healthfood side to his business several years ago, and has many other strings to his bow, so we depend on him for a wide range of supplies.

I have mentioned that we buy a certain amount of our fruit and vegetables organically grown; each year we are able to buy more, and we would, ideally, like to use only organically grown fruit and vegetables for our own and our guests' consumption. Now that we no longer grow our own herbs, we get an abundance of herbs by post each week from the excellent herb growers, Scots-herbs, at Errol in Perthshire.

Our cheese also comes by post, and for this we use Datapost (getting good produce when you live on an island is of necessity a very costly business). Until his recent retirement, we ordered it from Trevor Knowles, of

Above: A fishing boat at Ullapool.
Right: The Cuillins, a range of jagged black mountains,
on the Isle of Skye seen here in winter.

Moffat in Dumfriesshire, whom I consider to be one of the greatest authorities on cheese in Scotland today. He would supply us with three or four cheeses – one or two soft and creamy, one hard cheese, and Stilton – all made from unpasteurized milk, all delicious and perfect.

Our game – and some of our fish – comes from Duncan Fraser, the game dealer in Inverness, while most of our fish comes from George Lawrie, in Mallaig. Our meat comes from two sources: Mr Surtees, of Elgol, our excellent butcher, who delivers to us; but for Highland cattle beef we go to Michael Gibson at Macbeth's butcher's shop in Forres. Highland cattle beef is the most delicious kind, never killed when the beast is under 24 months old, and I shall be telling you about how these animals are raised, fed and hung, in a later chapter.

At Kinloch we offer a small menu: a choice of two first courses, followed by soup (Scotland is renowned for its soups); then two main courses, one of which is generally fish, with potatoes and two other vegetables; and a choice of two puddings. When planning the menus I try to balance the food, so that guests can choose between a rich and creamy pudding, for example a coffee and almond meringue, and an altogether lighter and fruitier pudding, for example fresh orange and Cointreau jelly with orange, grape and ginger compote. Our cheeses are laid out on the sideboard, with biscuits, and sticks of celery in a carved ivory vase, so that our guests can help themselves to as much or as little as they feel like, and

either before or after their pudding, as they wish. After dinner we serve coffee and fudge in both drawing-rooms; this gives those of our guests who smoke a chance to do so, because we ask guests not to smoke in the dining-room, in the interests of non-smokers.

Breakfasts are as important as dinner in our opinion. Scotland used to be famous for its breakfasts, and I find it very sad these days when one comes across a hotel where they serve 'continental breakfast' because no one, to my way of thinking, comes to Scotland for a continental breakfast. We make pinhead oatmeal porridge each evening for breakfast the following morning (it has to be started the previous evening), and we set out on the sideboard bowls of stewed rhubarb, dried figs in an orange-based syrup, and prunes, also stewed in orange. We have jugs of yoghurt, our own mixed muesli, and jugs of freshly squeezed orange juice. We bake scones each morning, and make toast with our own bread – we make six loaves of granary bread every day. We have kippers from Mallaig, finnan haddock when we can get it (there is no substitute for proper finnan haddock and we would rather not serve it at all than serve the little fillets of smoked haddock, which are dreary by comparison), black and white puddings, bacon – both smoked and unsmoked, kidneys, eggs, sausages and fried bread. After breakfast many of our guests say that they won't be able to eat another thing till dinner time, but it is surprising how peckish one becomes as the afternoon wears on, and we have a number of cakes and biscuits to serve with tea as guests come back from walks and excursions, or for new arrivals. Scotland is noted for its baking, and holidays after all are for self-indulgence, so we find that guests eat the tea-time items with relish – just the way I would, but try not to!

Lunch doesn't really feature here at Kinloch, unless a guest arrives early and asks for something, or the weather is particularly unspeakable and some guests choose to stay indoors and sit beside one of our two open fires with a book. Then they may feel like some soup or a sandwich, which we bring them on a tray by the fire.

Opposite: top left: Kinloch Lodge in winter.
Top right: Looking across the Sound of Sleat
from near Kinloch Lodge.
Bottom: The hilly terrain of the Isle of Raasay, with
the Cuillins of Skye in the background.

We have four children and, as I have already said, Kinloch is our family home. But we are fortunate enough to live separately from our guests. We have our own staircase and, although we are in the same house, we live quite independently. I think this is vital for both our guests' sakes and our own – people who come here on holiday searching for peace and quiet don't want to be disturbed by our children, and we feel immensely lucky to live in such a beautiful place without the restrictions we would have to impose on our children if we lived in a more integrated way with our guests. So it is ideal from every point of view.

The price you pay for living with so much space and peace around you is that to go anywhere necessitates a lengthy car journey, and the mileage we clock up would make most people wince. An added penalty is the ferry. We always use the Kyleakin to Kyle crossing, which is a 25-minute drive from here, and only a four-minute crossing, but each year during the summer months the ferry queues seem to become longer, and strategy becomes vital in planning trips off the island. There is much debate currently over whether or not there is to be a bridge linking us with the mainland. Perhaps by the time this book is published a decision will finally have been made, but what virtually all Skye people are agreed on, whether they are or are not in favour of a bridge in principle, is that it must not be a heavy toll bridge, which is what is being mooted at the moment. I must say, a bridge would make life very much easier and, with the ferry queues as they are these days, I really don't think that Skye would lose its island mystique if residents and visitors alike crossed over the sea to Skye by bridge rather than Caledonian MacBrayne ferry.

First-time visitors to the island (we much prefer the word visitor to the word tourist) are often taken aback by the size of Skye, which is indeed a very large island. Skye measures over six hundred square miles, and to drive from the topmost tip to the southerly end takes nearly three hours, but nowhere are you more than four miles from the sea, the coastline resembling that of Norway with its numerous inlets and fjords. Surprisingly, in spite of its large area, Skye has only eight-and-a-half thousand residents. I'm very glad that we are among them, and that we live the life we do. You can hardly call running a hotel a job – a way of life would be much more accurate, and it is one which suits both Godfrey and me admirably.

Oatcakes made with pinhead oatmeal.

OATCAKES

I used to think that making oatcakes was beyond me, that really only a born Scot could turn out edible ones (I'm English, just married to a Scot). But this recipe makes very good oatcakes and it is foolproof. If I can make them, anyone can! We use a coarse oatmeal – pinhead.

Makes about 35–40

8oz / 1½ cups / 225g self-raising flour
1 tsp bicarbonate of soda (baking soda)
1 tsp salt
1lb / 2⅔ cups / 450g pinhead oatmeal
(coarse Scotch oats)
5oz / 1¼ sticks / 150g butter or
margarine
3fl oz / 90ml each water and
milk mixed together

Sift the flour, soda and salt into a bowl and stir in the oatmeal. Rub the butter or margarine into the dry ingredients, then stir in the milk and water mixture. Sift some extra flour on to a table or work surface, and roll out the dough. Cut into rounds about 2 inches / 5cm in diameter, and carefully lift them on to a baking sheet.

Bake in a preheated moderate oven (350°F / 180°C / gas 4) until pale golden brown, 10–12 minutes. Cool on a wire rack. When the oatcakes are quite cold, store them in an airtight container.

To freshen up oatcakes which have been kept for several days, heat them on a baking sheet in a moderate oven for 5 minutes – they taste slightly toasted and delicious.

RICH FRUIT CAKE

There is nothing like a piece of really good fruit cake with a cup of tea or with a bit of cheese at a picnic. Fruit cakes are so convenient, in that they are much improved for being made several days, or better still weeks, in advance – providing, that is, that they are made with butter and not with margarine, and that they contain a good amount of alcohol, as mine do. Fruit cakes are amenable to changes, too – within reason, you can adjust the ingredients to suit your own personal likes and dislikes. If you can't stand glacé cherries, leave them out, but substitute another ingredient such as chopped dried apricots, for example, or increase the amount of sultanas or raisins.

Makes a 10 inch / 25cm cake

10oz / 2 cups / 300g plain
(all-purpose) flour
2 tsp ground ginger
½ tsp freshly grated nutmeg
2 tsp mixed spice (apple pie spice)
2 tsp ground cinnamon
8 oz / 1½ cups / 225g sultanas
(golden raisins)
8oz / 1½ cups / 225g raisins
12oz / 2⅔ cups / 350g currants
4oz / ⅔ cup / 120g chopped mixed
candied peel
4oz / ⅔ cup / 120g glacé cherries,
chopped
4 pieces of preserved ginger, chopped
6oz / 1½ cups / 175g prunes,
stoned and chopped
6oz / 1½ cups / 175g flaked (sliced)
almonds, toasted
10oz / 2½ sticks / 300g butter
10oz / 2 cups / 300g soft dark
brown sugar
grated rind and juice of 2 lemons
and 1 orange
5 size 2 / US extra large eggs, beaten
¼ pint / ⅔ cup / 150ml brandy, whisky,
sherry or rum

Grease a deep 10 inch / 25cm cake tin and line with baking parchment. Sift the flour and spices into a large bowl and add the fruit and nuts, mixing in well with your hands to coat all the fruit with flour. In another bowl, beat the butter until softened, then gradually beat in the sugar. Beat in the grated lemon and orange rinds. Add the fruit and nut mixture alternately with the eggs, beating all together well with a wooden spoon. Lastly, stir in the brandy, whisky, sherry or rum.

Put the mixture into the prepared cake tin, and make a hollow in the centre of the cake with the back of the wooden spoon. Bake in a preheated moderate oven (350°F / 180°C / gas 4) for 30 minutes, then reduce the temperature to 300°F / 150°C / gas 2 and bake for a further 2 hours. The cake is cooked when the sides are just beginning to come away from the tin, and when a sharp knife or skewer stuck in the middle of the cake comes out clean.

Take the cake out of the oven and let it cool completely in the tin before turning it out and wrapping it well in a double thickness of foil.

OVEN SCONES

We make scones like these every day at Kinloch Lodge — for ourselves and the guests. They are much nicer made and eaten straight away.

Makes 20–24 scones

1½lb / 4¾ cups / 700g self-raising flour
1 tsp salt
2 rounded tsp baking powder
2 tbsp golden (light corn) syrup
2 size 1 / US extra large eggs, beaten
2 tbsp sunflower oil
about ¾ pint / 2 cups / 450ml milk
(to make 1 pint / 2½ cups / 600ml when combined with eggs)

Sift the flour, salt and baking powder into a large mixing bowl. Mix together the syrup, beaten eggs, sunflower oil and milk, and gradually add this to the dry ingredients.

Flour a tabletop or work surface, and tip the dough on to it. With floured hands, pat the dough smooth, patting it out to a thickness of about 1 inch / 2·5cm — the dough is too damp to roll out with a rolling pin satisfactorily. Cut into circles with a scone or other cutter, and put the scones on a baking sheet.

Bake in a preheated hot oven, (425°F / 220°C / gas 7) for 12–15 minutes. Serve warm.

KINLOCH MARMALADE

How I love making marmalade. Each January I get more than a chance to indulge my passion as I have to make literally hundreds of pounds of marmalade to last us and our guests throughout the coming year. There is something very satisfying about seeing the finished rows of jars in the larder, and I often take myself in there for a gloat – and to spur me on when, after making several batches, even I am beginning to tire of it! The lovely smell of marmalade simmering is an added incentive. The quantities given here make just the right amount – if you try to make more, it becomes difficult to get a set.

Makes 8–10 lb / 3·6–4·5kg

3lb / 1·4kg Seville oranges
3lb / 1·4kg other citrus fruit such as lemons, limes, grapefruit and sweet oranges, tangerines or clementines (never dreary and tasteless satsumas)
8 pints / 5 quarts / 4·5 litres water
12lb / 5·4kg granulated or preserving sugar

Scrub all the fruit in hot soapy water to get rid of as much as possible of the horrendous preservatives with which they are often sprayed; rinse well. Put the fruit into a preserving pan (kettle) or a large saucepan with the water, and bring the water to the boil. Cover the pan with a lid and simmer very gently for 3–4 hours.

Take the pan off the heat when the fruit looks pulpy, and cool them enough to be able to handle them without pain. Take each piece of fruit out of the liquid, cut it in half and scoop any pips into a small saucepan. Put the fruit into a food processor and whiz briefly to cut it up, but take care not to purée it; I find this easiest done if I process the fruit in small amounts. Put the whizzed fruit back into the large saucepan. Set aside.

Add 1 pint / 2½ cups / 600ml water to the pips and simmer them gently for 20 minutes, then strain this water (full of

natural pectin) through a sieve into the contents of the large pan. Add the sugar to the marmalade mixture and, over moderate heat, stir to dissolve the sugar, taking great care not to let the marmalade boil before the sugar has completely dissolved – you will feel a gritty texture with your wooden spoon as you stir. When all the sugar has dissolved, let the marmalade mixture come to a full and rolling boil, and boil it fast for 20–25 minutes, watching to be sure it does not boil over the top of the pan.

Pull the pan off the heat and trickle some of the hot marmalade on to a saucer. Leave for several minutes to cool, then push the surface with your fingertip – if it wrinkles, you have a set and you can pot the marmalade into warmed jars, seal and label. If it doesn't wrinkle, put the pan back on the heat and boil fast for another 5 minutes before testing for a set once more. The longer the marmalade boils, the darker will be the result, so it is good to get a set at the earliest opportunity. Store the jars in a cool space.

A favourite family photograph of Godfrey's grandmother, Helen Banks.

ESTABLISHMENTS

—— OF ——

DISTINCTION

Altnaharrie Inn, Ross-shire
The Dower House, Ross-shire
Polmaily House Hotel, Inverness-shire
Inverlochy Castle, Fort William
Ardsheal House, Argyll
Pittodrie House Hotel, Aberdeenshire
Cringletie House Hotel, Peebles-shire
The Peat Inn, Fife
Airds Hotel, Argyll
Valvona and Crolla, Edinburgh

*Opposite: The massive chandelier and painted ceiling
in the drawing-room of Inverlochy Castle.
Above: Detail from a painting at Pittodrie House Hotel.*

*Altnaharrie Inn is set on the south shore of Loch Broom
and reached by their own ferry in ten minutes from Ullapool.*

THERE IS nowhere quite like Altnaharrie. This is due partly to its splendid location, across Loch Broom from Ullapool, and partly to its owners. For those who don't know the north-west coast, Loch Broom is a wide loch, and it takes fully ten minutes to cross over from the jetty at Ullapool in *Mother Goose*, the hotel's boat. Altnaharrie is an old drover's inn, dating from the eighteenth century or earlier, but it has been a very special small hotel since 1980. It is owned and run by Fred Brown, from Hamilton, who is a vet by training, and his Norwegian wife Gunn Eriksen. It is the combination of Fred and Gunn, together with Altnaharrie's location, which makes it such a very special place to stay, and to eat.

The food is like nowhere else in Great Britain. Gunn, an artist by training, is also an artist of taste and flavour. She combines wild berries and even plants we think of as weeds, such as nettles and chickweed, with all the very best fish and shellfish, game and meat. Not only is the food at Altnaharrie exquisite, it is also exquisitely served. In the dining-room, which consists of two rooms knocked into one, the tables are immaculately set, with a flower tucked into each napkin, and with antique glasses. At dinner there is a set menu with no choice until the pudding course, when there are three choices, although choice isn't exactly the right word because Fred gently encourages each guest to eat all three. He has an easy time with me – I need no encouragement whatever! Unusual combinations, like nettle and brie soup, for example, prove quite delicious. Ravioli containing scallops, lobster, prawns and crab with a champagne sauce, could well be followed by medallions of Sika deer, or a pigeon breast with juniper among the ingredients of its accompanying sauce. Gunn's sauces are delicately flavoured, yet always impact-making, and always perfectly complementary to the dishes with which they are served. This is what I mean by Gunn's artistry being in her cooking. Her puddings are the stuff dreams are made from. Indeed, I often dream of a Norwegian Cream Cake I ate at Altnaharrie more than five years ago. It was composed of the thinnest layers of the lightest sponge with a fruity cream between each layer, and the whole encased in paper-thin marzipan. Her cloudberry ice-cream in a biscuit tuile, her rhubarb tart, with its meltingly crumbly pastry, her rich chocolate cake – whatever Gunn makes is utterly delectable. And if it sounds as though I'm going overboard and getting carried away in gutsy reminiscences, I am, unashamedly! At breakfast, once again the tables are exquisitely set with glazed pottery.

Fred and Gunn have recently enlarged Altnaharrie, by building into the hillside behind the original house. This gives a second, large and very attractive sitting-room at first-floor level – the other one is downstairs, warm and cosy with its open fire, and the perfect place to curl up with a book. There are eight bedrooms, some fairly small, which encourages me because most of our own bedrooms are small here at Kinloch. But the Altnaharrie bedrooms are as exquisitely furnished as the dining-room tables are set, with every possible thing you could want, and each has its own luxurious bathroom. The electricity at Altnaharrie is from a generator, which is switched off after midnight when all the guests have gone to bed, but there is ample warning for all the guests, and this somehow adds to the personality and attraction of the hotel.

At Altnaharrie there is literally nothing to do except to walk, or to read by a fire when the weather is inclement. There are wonderful walks up the hill behind the house, and over towards Little Loch Broom, the next loch over the hill. Of course, you can always take the *Mother Goose* across to Ullapool – back to reality, as I think of it when I leave Altnaharrie – and the wonderful Inverewe Gardens are within easy reach. They were laid out by Osgood MacKenzie during the latter part of the nineteenth century, and are now the property of the National Trust for Scotland, who maintain the gardens beautifully. But when I'm at Altnaharrie I like to stay

This view across Loch Broom from the Inn gives an idea of beautiful walks to be had in the area.

remote and just walk – time there passes all too quickly anyway. Outside the house there are ducks and fowl pottering about but these belong to Fred and Gunn and are certainly not destined for the table. Beachcombers can wander along the shore of the loch, which is pebbles and shingles rather than sand, and watch the extremely hard work that goes into running such a faultless place as Altnaharrie, which appears to be so effortlessly run, and yet for which every last thing, including the kerosene for the generator, must be brought over from Ullapool by boat and carried up the slipway. Life is certainly not easy for Fred and Gunn, but, oh, how wonderful it is to stay there, to feel one is truly away from everything, and to enjoy Fred and Gunn's peaceful company – for they are the most attentive and yet the most discreet of hosts.

THE DOWER HOUSE

JUST NORTH of Inverness is the Black Isle, a large, triangular promontory almost surrounded by the waters of the Moray, Cromarty and Beauly Firths. Here, a mile outside the village of Muir of Ord, is the Dower House, a small hotel run by Robyn and Mena Aitchison. When you turn in past the green and white painted railings the driveway leads you through the gardens surrounding the house, wide lawns and a variety of beautiful trees, planted some two hundred years ago, when the house was built. The Dower House is a low, one-storey, cottage orné style building – one of those architectural eccentricities you come across in Scotland. It is tempting to exclaim over its prettiness, within and without, but that would be to give too twee an image. It is an enchanting house, and lovely in its unusualness.

Inside, it feels more like a home than a hotel. There are five bedrooms, each with its own bathroom, and each decorated with beautiful fabrics in glowing and vibrant colours. The corridors leading from the front of the house to the bedrooms are papered in silk marble-effect apricot, bright yet elegant, and in keeping with the house. The drawing-room leads off the hall, and it manages to be cosy yet elegant, with apricot sponged-effect wallpaper, a log fire, and chintzy comfortable chair-coverings as well as a dark blue silky sofa. There is a window seat in the low-ceilinged bay window, ideal for curling up and reading the magazines and books which are scattered around. The hall is papered in apricot and plum-

Below: The exterior and garden of the Dower House just outside the village of Muir of Ord.
Right: A table setting in the elegant dining room.

coloured striped paper, and leads into the dining-room, which is papered in plum. Throughout the house the furniture consists of antiques, interesting as well as beautiful – including an exquisite Grandmother clock in the hall.

The Dower House originally belonged to nearby Highfield House, the home of the Mackenzie-Gillanders family. Like many such houses all over Britain, it was designed to be the home of the dowager, the widow of the head of the family. The link with the Mackenzies is reflected in the use of Mackenzie tartan ribbon which ties together the pages of the hand-written wine list, and which is also used to tie up each dark green table napkin. The long dining-room has a log fire at one end, polished tables, and in one corner a table covered in a lace cloth holds an array of liqueur bottles. Dinner is served for a maximum of fifteen people, the number most comfortably accommodated both in the dining-room and in the drawing-room before and after dinner. The menu consists of a choice of two first courses, plus soup, a choice of two main courses, and a choice of two puddings, with cheese either before or after the pudding.

Although the Aitchisons have only been running the Dower House as a hotel for a year, they are well known in the North of Scotland from the days when they owned the renowned French restaurant, Le Chardon, in nearby Cromarty. Robyn was previously manager of the Ballachulish hotel, at Loch Leven, for six years before he and Mena, a former radiographer, bought the Dower House and the restaurant, Le Chardon. To finance the renovation of the house, Robyn worked on an offshore oil rig for four years, using his two weeks off each month for working on the house and creating the restaurant. Their food ideas from their Le Chardon days have been carried through to the Dower House. They search continually for the best fresh and, where possible, local produce. Robyn, who is the cook, is self-taught and gets his inspiration partly from recipe books and partly from his imagination.

The Aitchisons have done a magnificent job at the Dower House, which deserves to be recognized as a gem among Scotland's small hotels. It is a lovely old house, furnished and decorated with good taste and at great expense. Like the other hoteliers in this book, the Aitchisons are dedicated to their work and their way of life, and are helping to promote all that is best in Scotland.

POLMAILY HOUSE HOTEL

IF, AS you approach Inverness from the west, you turn left in Drumnadrochit, on to the A831 road to Cannich, after approximately three miles you come to a sign on the right saying Polmaily House Hotel. At the top of a drive, lined with tall beech hedges, you arrive at a white-painted Edwardian house. Polmaily is set on the slopes of Glenurqhuart and surrounded by beautiful gardens. In front and to one side of the house there is a pond (the home of many ducks), and there is also a tennis court and a vegetable garden. Beyond the house there is a swimming pool, with trees nearby. Inside, Polmaily feels like a house rather than a hotel. The drawing-room has a log fire, there are the comfy armchairs covered in chintzy stuff, and throughout the house there are pictures, bowls of flowers from the garden, pretty and interesting ornaments, piles of books and bits and pieces dotted around the rooms, all of which contribute to the relaxed atmosphere.

Nick and Alison Parsons have lived at Polmaily since 1982, and from early April to mid October they open their home as a hotel. Before 1982 Nick worked for Reuters and they lived all over the world. They did two stints in Rome, one in Dar es Salaam, and finally a couple of years in Mexico. While they were abroad Alison used to do semi-professional work cooking for embassy lunches and dinners, and developing her love for and interest in foreign food. It was during their ten years overseas that their two children were born. As the children grew older, Nick and Alison decided to return to Britain, and they went to live in Nick's family home in the New Forest, while Nick was working as editor of *Yachting World*. After a couple of years, with both children away at school, they started to look for a business where they could work together, and decided that the ideal thing would be a hotel in Scotland. It had to be in Scotland where Alison comes from, and preferably in the Highlands. It had to have a Granny flat for Nick's mother. Because they wanted to run a hotel with a restaurant, it had to be near a catchment area. They looked at several hotels before they saw Polmaily advertised in the *Daily Telegraph*.

It fitted all the Parsons' requirements perfectly, and

Opposite: Polmaily is a peaceful country house which stands in its own lovely grounds. Its setting, surrounded by beautiful gardens on the slopes of Glenurquhart, is outstanding.

its situation is ideal: for dinner visitors it is within easy reach of Inverness, for their residential guests, within exploring range of Aviemore, Cawdor and Culloden to the east, and Skye, Inverewe, Ullapool and Lochinver to the west. The Granny flat meant that Nick's mother could move north with them and yet maintain her independence. She is an invaluable member of the team, as she is responsible for all reservations and for answering the telephone. Every couple running a hotel could do with such an ally in the family!

They started with an *à la carte* menu which usually consisted of about seven first courses, five main courses, and four or five puddings. In 1989, faced with the choice of putting up their prices or altering their menu format, they opted for the latter and have based their menu on the French notion of a basic three-course menu at a fixed price, or with a slightly more elaborate four-course, and a five-course menu available at higher prices. Alison thrives on the variety of cooking involved with her menus. She has four assistants one of whom cooks with her each night at the height of the season, three of whom are also involved with preparation work in the mornings. Alison cooks breakfast each morning for the guests, and she finds the hard slog of her kitchen work infinitely preferable to the occasions when she gets involved in front-of-house work, usually on Nick's night off.

Alison's love of cooking and deep interest in food means that they are continually searching for reliable suppliers. These days their supplies come from far and near. Nearest probably is the Fassock Farm, from whom the Parsons get quail's eggs and fresh and smoked quails. Lancashire-based Brayhead Foods supplies them with fresh duck, corn-fed chicken, and also with their cheeses; they love to experiment with their cheeses, and when I saw them recently they were positively raving about a cheese from Ireland new to them this year, called Cashel Blue. They were also raving, or rather puzzling, over why the *Good Food Guide* had knocked a point off Polmaily's rating. No reason had been given, and they themselves felt that the hotel was better than ever, with better and more reliable supplies. We agreed that inspectors for various guides can only be a pretty jaundiced lot. What *really* matters, as Nick and Alison summed up, is to have happy guests who return each year, and to have enquiries and reservations from new guests — on the recommendation of previous ones. I couldn't agree with them more.

So MUCH has been written about Inverlochy that you might think there can be no more to be said. Every guide-book contains paeons of praise to this wonderful hotel near Fort William. In fact, if anything detrimental is written about Inverlochy, I tend to assume it is the writer who is suspect. The only thing which the reports sometimes fail to mention is the friendliness of the staff. Surely this is one of the most important things, but one which the writers perhaps feel is at odds with their descriptions of the formality and splendour to be found at Inverlochy. For me, it is the friendliness and total lack of servility and obsequiousness which makes Inverlochy unique among the truly grand hotels in Britain today. This atmosphere and attitude emanate from its owner, Grete Hobbs, and the managing director, Michael Leonard.

Inverlochy Castle was bought in 1944 by Mrs Hobbs's father-in-law, a Canadian industrialist. Previously one of the properties of Lord Abinger, Inverlochy had housed Commandoes on training exercises during the Second World War. It was the Scottish home of the Hobbs family (who also live in Leicestershire), until its transformation into a hotel in 1969. Even the wildest enthusiast could never describe Inverlochy as a house of great beauty or architectural interest. Rather it is a solid, typically Scottish baronial castle. A discreet black and white sign at the side of the main road between Fort William and Spean Bridge

Previous pages: Inverlochy Castle, a nineteenth-century baronial mansion, standing in the shadow of Ben Nevis. Below: The comfortable and welcoming drawing-room.

directs the visitor to Inverlochy up a long drive through beautiful gardens, full of spectacular redwood trees. There is a porticoed entrance, giving welcome protection when the weather is inclement – which is a polite way of describing some of the weather we get in Scotland.

Mrs Hobbs, who is Danish by birth, is a charming, elegant woman with a warm personality. The interior of Inverlochy is a reflection of her excellent taste. There is a large hall, leading into a vast room with a fireplace, sofas and chairs – and a spectacular view of Ben Nevis. Leading off it are the two dining-rooms, and the impressive and elegant drawing-room, which has a view over the rhododendron-covered gardens to the lake. This room has a grand piano, Louis Quinze furniture, beautiful lamps and mirrors, and photographs of the Hobbs family, all of which maintain the original atmosphere of the family home it once was.

The dining-rooms are comfortable, with tables spaced far enough apart to ensure privacy, and they are immaculate in every detail from the silver to the crystal. Inverlochy has always been renowned for its food, from the early days of the legendary Miss Shaw who was the cook from the hotel's opening in 1969 till her retirement in 1982. The food was indeed wonderful – I particularly remember her orange soufflés, and raspberry *crème brûlée*. After Miss Shaw's retirement (when she was awarded the MBE) Mrs Hobbs and Michael Leonard went to consult Michel Bourdin of the Connaught Hotel in London about a chef to take her place, and on his recommendation François Huguet took over the kitchen. Michel Bourdin was also instrumental in introducing Graham Newbould, who succeeded Huguet as head chef in 1986. The method used by Mrs Hobbs and Michael Leonard in their search for the right chef was to eat in the restaurant where the prospective chef currently worked, to judge his food for themselves. In Graham's case this test was impossible because at the time he was chef for the Prince and Princess of Wales, at Kensington Palace. So he was invited to Inverlochy to cook a trial meal. He arrived in the evening, to cook lunch the following day, never having been in the kitchen before. He cooked a seafood brioche, roast rack of lamb, and raspberry soufflé – and one assumes it was a delicious meal.

Graham Newbould is an excellent cook. A quiet, shy and unassuming man, he looks much younger than his 33 years. Graham had no idea of what he wanted to do after leaving school, and certainly had no aspirations to be a chef until, two weeks before he left, his careers master told him of a spare place on a year's catering course, in his native Yorkshire, and he took it. His first job was in the Leeds Crest Motel, which he says seemed to him the acme of haute cuisine at the time. From there he worked in small hotels in Yorkshire and Lancashire before moving to London. For the first year in London he worked at the Connaught, and he then went to work at Buckingham Palace. During his time working for the Royal Family (throughout which he appreciated the family atmosphere) he worked at Sandringham, Balmoral and Holyrood Palace, ending up working at Kensington Palace for four and a half years.

Although Graham produces such wonderful, grand food at Inverlochy, he says that his favourite cooking is his mother's. This is perfect for Inverlochy because if, as frequently happens, a guest requests some traditional British dish such as steak and kidney pudding, Graham can cook it to the same perfection as the other more elaborate food he creates. He loves working at Inverlochy, he says, and he is aware of the excitement of working in Scotland, where there is a real enthusiasm for cooking and eating, and he feels this is especially true in hotels and restaurants in the West of Scotland. He gets his supplies from all over Britain. Of his fruit and vegetables, for example, some come from the extensive kitchen gardens at Inverlochy, some from Jacki Buchan in nearby Morar, and every Friday a consignment arrives from France.

Michael Leonard, the managing director of Inverlochy, is a quiet Irishman with a wonderful sense of humour. He and Mrs Hobbs have a unique working relationship. He arrived at Inverlochy in 1976, after a hotel training in France, Germany and Switzerland. Until 1976 Mrs Hobbs had spent all of each summer at Inverlochy managing the hotel entirely herself, while her family divided their time between their homes in Leicestershire and Inverlochy. About a year earlier, Michael was working in a private members' dining club in Leicestershire. He had left the Continent to work in London, which he loathed, and had taken the job in Leicestershire as a temporary post before returning to Switzerland. It was at the club that he first met the Hobbs family, coincidentally having dinner with the Earl of Lanesborough, a cousin of my husband, who also lives in

Leicestershire. Michael was telephoned by Peter, Mrs Hobbs' son, and at his request he went to see the family at their home, where they invited him to work at Inverlochy. However, Michael refused the invitation, and about that time he married Muriel, whom he had met while working at the club. From time to time the invitation to work at Inverlochy was renewed, and after a year Mrs Hobbs issued an ultimatum: either he accepted the job or she would advertise the position nationally. Michael's reason for refusing up till now was that he feared that he wouldn't have enough to occupy him at Inverlochy, but on receiving the ultimatum he accepted, partly because of the prospect of good fishing as a bonus – and next to his family and Inverlochy, fishing is his passion.

Michael is the linchpin of the day-to-day running of Inverlochy. When he is interviewing prospective employees he doesn't look for skills, because those he can teach himself. What he does look for is personality and the ability to smile. He likes people to be responsive and able to state their views, and it is this which I'm sure accounts for the lack of servility and obsequiousness at Inverlochy.

Inverlochy is a member of the prestigious Châteaux et Relais – one of only three members in Scotland – and the grand reputation of this legendary hotel is fully deserved. To stay at Inverlochy, as any guest will tell you, is an unforgettable experience.

Although the exterior of Inverlochy is imposing, the atmosphere inside the castle is warm and welcoming. Below: A detail from one of the elegant fireplaces.

ARDSHEAL HOUSE

ARDSHEAL HOUSE, the house featured in Robert Louis Stevenson's *Kidnapped*, is now a thriving hotel, and run by an American couple, Bob and Jane Taylor. The story of how they came to find and buy Ardsheal, and change their whole lives in midstream, is a fascinating one. It was in 1976 that they saw a sign on the main Oban to Fort William road saying 'ARDSHEAL HOUSE, FOR SALE'. They had always spent their holidays in Scotland, and had a special love for the West Coast, and the Loch Linnhe area in particular. They decided to turn off the main road and have a snoop at this house which was for sale. They followed the very long single-track road which is the drive to Ardsheal, and which curves around the coast, through beautiful old trees, till they came upon the house.

Originally built in 1500, Ardsheal was burnt down in the Rebellion of 1745, and rebuilt in 1760. It stands in an extraordinarily beautiful garden, a cultivated garden immediately around the house, with a steep hill rising at the back. In front of the house a wide sweep of land, planted with more of the rare and wonderful trees which surround Ardsheal for miles (and which were planted by the grandfather of Neil Sutherland, a former owner of Ardsheal House), provides as lovely a panorama as you could hope to see, including the shore of Loch Linnhe and the hills of Morvern.

Bob and Jane were shown over the house by the then owner, an English lady, who ran Ardsheal like a glorified bed and breakfast. Having had a good look around, they went back to the Ballachulish Hotel, where they were staying, and sat up for half the night discussing the meaning of life and the pattern of their lives, and how the

Ardsheal House at Kentallen, originally built for the Stewarts of Appin,
is situated on a beautiful peninsular and makes the perfect West-coast base.

*The Taylors keep Indian Runner ducks for
showing and for eggs, strictly not for the table.*

future could turn out. The next day they returned to Ardsheal, found they were both in love with it, and returned to America to give up their jobs there – Bob was Vice President of Morgan Bank, and Jane was Vice President and Creative Director of a large New York advertising agency. They put their Manhattan town house on the market, and enrolled their two sons, then aged thirteen and fifteen, in boarding school, packed three container loads of possessions and shipped them over to Ardsheal. They say they were on a high the whole time!

On returning to Ardsheal they set about tackling the task of turning it into the sort of hotel they would like to stay in themselves. At the beginning there were only three bathrooms in the entire house, and each room had string pull light switches to a centre bulb. The furniture was what Jane describes as 1950s airport – bright plastic with screw-in chrome legs. Now, Ardsheal has twelve double bedrooms and one single, each with its own bathroom, and the furniture and paintings are antique.

The house is big and comfortable, with a large sitting-hall, with a huge fireplace, and two smaller sitting-rooms off, all comfortably furnished. The hall is where coffee is served after dinner, and it makes a convivial meeting-point for the guests. In addition to the main dining-room there is a large conservatory dining-room, light and airy, leading off it. The gardens, where two gardeners are employed, are immaculate, and provide much of the fruit and vegetables used in the kitchen. The food at Ardsheal is exquisite, using the best of local prod-

uce combined imaginatively with herbs. I can remember everything I've ever eaten at Ardsheal, and there can be no greater compliment!

Less than fifty per cent of Bob and Jane's guests are from the United States. The proportion used to be higher, but the number of British and European guests has increased. On several occasions the whole house has been taken over by a family for a special birthday or anniversary celebration, and Bob and Jane love these occasions, when they organize boat trips, and arrange for Frank Clark to come over from his Whisky Centre to give a talk on whisky – and a tasting.

Bob and Jane are great fun, tremendous hosts, and they have their lives cleverly arranged – nine months of being hoteliers in one of the most beautiful places in Scotland, and three months spent in their farmhouse in New Paltz, halfway up the Hudson River, between New York City and Albany. Incidentally, their farmhouse was built in 1750, and is therefore older than the oldest part of Ardsheal. They reckon that, with their life of contrasts, they have the perfect recipe for living.

An important part of their life at Ardsheal, incidentally, is their gentle Scottish deerhound, Dram. When they are in America, she stays with Pat Aird at her famous kennels near Ayr. In 1989, Dram gave birth to two daughters, of whom they kept one, and the other now lives with us at Kinloch – so there is a definite relationship, transcending mere friendship, between the Taylors and the Macdonalds!

*A selection of fresh herbs, framed by variegated
ivy, from Ardsheal's own garden.*

PITTODRIE HOUSE HOTEL

The drawing-room at Pittodrie House Hotel which has been in the family for nearly one hundred years.

PITTODRIE IS beautifully situated, at the foot of Bennachie, in the depths of rural farming countryside in Aberdeenshire, between Aberdeen and Huntly. The oldest bits of the house date back to 1490, when the original house was built. This was burnt down by Montrose in the time of the Covenanters, and the house was rebuilt in 1675. Pittodrie originally belonged to the Erskine family, but that particular branch of the family died out and the house was bought in 1898 by the grandfather of the present owner, Theo Smith.

The house is filled with fine antiques and portraits – wherever you look your gaze falls on something of interest or beauty, usually both. The big front door opens into a circular hall in which there are four niches, each holding a French bronze figure of near life size, depicting Spring, Summer, Autumn and Winter. The long drawing-room opens off this circular hall, and it has windows facing two directions, those at the far end giving spectacular views to the south, the others giving on to the front. This lovely, dark red room has numerous comfortable but elegant chairs and sofas, and a large fireplace with a handsome wood mantel carved with grapes – a motif which I have noticed also in the panelling around the Elphinstone Hall of Aberdeen University. The drawing-room contains glass display cabinets full of antique china and glass.

From the attractive circular hall you proceed into the main hall, where there is a reception desk tucked away to one side – the only indication that this isn't a private house but a hotel. On one wall in the large inner hall hangs a vast and beautiful creamy white embroidered Persian bedspread, which used to belong to Theo Smith's grandmother. It is now safely behind glass. Beside it is the door into the blue dining-room, another elegant room with huge portraits. The inner hall leads past the staircase and into narrower corridors, past the oldest bits of the original 1490 house, and to a billiard room. Even here there are distractions for would-be billiards players: in one corner of the room there is the oldest perambulator I have ever seen, and on the deep windowsills there are huge old chemists' jars filled with coloured water. The corridors are filled with display cases, containing work by local artists and craftsmen which can be purchased within the hotel. The walls are also hung with prints of Scottish subjects, all for sale at reasonable prices.

Theo Smith turned Pittodrie from a family home into a hotel in 1977. There is nothing remotely hotel-like about the feel of the house now, but it is an extremely busy hotel. So busy, in fact, that Theo has plans well underway to double the size, adding twelve new bedrooms to the twelve they already have, and these will be finished in 1990. He has bought old stone for the building, and has gone to great lengths to get a sympathetic architectural design, complete with turrets, for his new extension, so that it will blend in with the old house. The

The spectacular flower arrangements and delicious herbs at Pittodrie come from the peaceful and secluded garden.

Parts of Pittodrie House Hotel date back as far
as 1490, although the main part of the house was built in 1675.

bedrooms at Pittodrie are as individual as the downstairs rooms. They all have bathrooms en suite, many of them with 1920s fittings, wide baths, and spacious basins.

When Pittodrie first became a hotel Theo did the cooking himself. He is basically a self-taught cook, but has a real love of good food. Now Pittodrie is open all year round (with the exception of Christmas), and they have so many extra dinner guests in addition to residents that they employ a permanent chef, Robert Hughes. All the food is fresh and seasonal. They are very fortunate at Pittodrie in being able to get virtually all their supplies locally. The menu changes each night, with a choice of four first courses, three entrées, six main courses, and there is always a fine selection of puddings, which are brought to the table on a trolley.

Theo has over two hundred wines on his list, supplied by Irvine Robertson Wines and by Justerini and Brooks. They come from as far afield as Chile, Argentina, Rumania and Hungary, as well as from the more familiar wine-producing countries.

Pittodrie has a wonderful garden, which provides all the flowers for the spectacular flower arrangements throughout the house, as well as all the herbs used in the kitchen. Although peaceful and secluded, Pittodrie is extremely conveniently situated, being only forty minutes' drive from Aberdeen. Theo's guests are a mix of holiday-makers and business travellers, taking the opportunity to combine work with a chance to stay in comfort, in lovely surroundings, in a beautiful part of Scotland with all of the Dee and Donside virtually on the doorstep.

CRINGLETIE HOUSE

CRINGLETIE IS situated up a long drive off the main Peebles to Edinburgh road, about twenty miles south of Edinburgh. It is a very attractive house, built of soft pink Dumfries stone. The original house was built in 1666 but was knocked down after a second house was built in 1861 by David Bryce, the well-known Scottish architect, in a castellated, baronial style. One enters through a wide and attractive outer hallway, and one's immediate impression is that the house is full of oak. A wide oak staircase leads up to the first floor, where there are two dining-rooms, one on the front of the house, the other on the back. Both are beautiful rooms, and the views are spectacular from all four sides of Cringletie. Also on the first floor is the large oak-panelled drawing-room, with windows on two sides, and an interesting painted ceiling. Next to this room there is a small drawing-room, reserved for non-smokers. This pretty room, containing a marble fireplace with scallop-shell carvings, used to be the ladies' withdrawing room in the days when the house belonged to the Murray family. Cringletie belonged at one time to Colonel Alexander Murray, who accepted the surrender of Quebec after the death of General Wolfe.

In 1966 Cringletie was bought by an Edinburgh doctor and converted into a hotel. It has been in the hands of its present owners, Stanley and Aileen Maguire, since 1971. Until then, Stanley had been working with a pharmaceutical company in London. Aileen is English but already had Scottish connections, as her brother, Keith Knight, was the then owner of the prestigious Houstoun House hotel at Uphall, near Edinburgh. It was Keith Knight who first inspired the Maguires to look for a hotel to run in Scotland, and he also helped them to find Cringletie.

There are thirteen bedrooms at Cringletie, all comfortable and attractive, and each has its own bathroom. The whole interior is comfortably furnished, and the surroundings and views are spectacular. Cringletie is within easy reach of Edinburgh – about 45 minutes by car – and also within striking distance of such lovely Borders towns as Peebles and Kelso, with their gaunt/picturesque wool mills.

Many of the guests at Cringletie return each year, and one of the great attractions is Aileen Maguire's cooking. She has always had an interest in food and a love of cooking, and when she and Stanley arrived at Cringletie she set about tackling the problem of trying to find the best produce to enable her to give their guests the sort of food which they themselves would like to find. As we all found in our early days, this was not easy, not even for the Maguires, living within comparatively easy reach of Edinburgh. When she asked a leading Edinburgh fruit and vegetable supplier for fennel he seemed to be very negative – then he asked her if fennel was the vegetable which looked like a set of bagpipes! Now the gardens at Cringletie produce a great deal of their own vegetables and fruit, and Aileen makes jams and jellies which are attractively displayed for sale in crystal jars in the hallway. However, they are by no means self-sufficient, and the rest of their fruit and vegetables come from Ormerods, in Edinburgh.

These days the Maguires have solved their supply problems, and the only thing that is not easy for them to obtain is good fish. They have to collect their fish orders from an Edinburgh firm, Hughes & Sons, which makes me realize how lucky we west coast hoteliers are to have a ready supply of fresh fish. Having said that, I should add that I recently ate wonderful scampi at Cringletie, in a first course of a meltingly short pastry tartlet filled with scampi and covered with a Bearnaise sauce.

Aileen is a marvellous cook. She is small, vivacious and enthusiastic, and I would love to work with her. She is, however, ably assisted by Sheila McKellar. None of her staff had professional training, but they are all immensely efficient and help to create the happy and relaxed atmosphere that exists at Cringletie. Stanley and Aileen have three sons, of whom the eldest, Paul, is now working in the kitchen with Aileen and Sheila, while the second son, Simon, now works full-time in front of house.

As I've already said, a high proportion of the guests at Cringletie are returning visitors, which speaks volumes about the comfort, good food and warmth of welcome to be found there.

Opposite, top: Cringletie House is a handsome Victorian mansion, built in red sandstone and set well back from the road. Opposite, bottom left: Aileen Maguire's home-made redcurrant jelly.
Bottom right: A detail from the magnificent fireplace.

THE PEAT INN

Opposite: David Wilson, world-famous chef of the Peat Inn.
Above: Village dances were once held in this room.

THE MOST remarkable thing about the village called Peat Inn, in rural Fife, is the Peat Inn itself. Seventeen years ago David and Patricia Wilson bought the Peat Inn, which until then had been the village pub. A couple of years earlier, David's love of food and wine had led to his leaving his job and his normal life, as he puts it, as a marketing manager for one of the companies within the Rio Tinto Zinc Group. He then spent two years working in restaurants to gain experience before they began looking for a place of their own. Financial considerations dictated where they looked; cities were out of the question – it had to be in a rural area. The Peat Inn fitted the bill and gradually, over the years, the Wilsons converted and rebuilt it, making the original bar at the front of the house into a comfortable sitting-room where guests can now enjoy their drinks before dinner and coffee afterwards. The large room at the back, where village dances had been held, became the dining-room, with part of the room divided off to make a kitchen. By 1978 the inn was regarded as one of the best places to eat in Scotland – if not in the UK – and the Wilsons' reputation had grown to the extent that they began to contemplate whether they should buy a country house hotel, or a place in Edinburgh or Glasgow. In the end, however, they

decided to stay put and continue to embellish the Peat Inn, the advantages of being in a rural location outweighing the disadvantages. Not being in an urban area has spared them the hectic year-round trade pressures which a city location would undoubtedly bring; and they like the idea that people have to make an effort to visit the Peat Inn. Of course the prospect of travelling to a comparatively remote place in the middle of winter is enough to put many people off altogether, but the Wilsons welcome the space, peace and time to think which this allows them. They simply close down their operation for two weeks in November, when they go to France to rest, eat, drink and be inspired, and for the whole of January. They are also closed every Sunday.

In 1987 the Wilsons built and opened their Residence. This is an attractive one-storey building set back from the Inn, containing ten bedroom suites. When you open the front door of the Residence you find yourself in a hall cum sitting-room brightly decorated in red, blue and white, with a large stone fireplace facing you. It is a warm, welcoming room, where the smartness of the decor somehow manages not to conflict with the rural scenes outside. The bedroom suites are perfectly designed and appointed, with beautiful fabrics, any of which I would love to have at Kinloch. Breakfast is served in your suite at whatever time you choose between 8.00 and 10.30 a.m.

A copy of the Peat Inn wine list is in each of the bedroom suites, and it makes for an absorbing half-hour's reading. The list is a reflection of David Wilson's love of wine and fascination with the subject – he describes wine as his hobby. There are over four hundred wines – excluding the champagnes – with the white wines printed on white paper, and the red on pink paper. David has built up so many contacts that people now come to him, if they know of interesting rarities.

At the Peat Inn there are three types of menu: a fixed-price tasting menu, containing small amounts of those dishes for which the Peat Inn is renowned; a menu of the day, also fixed-price, with no choice at each of its six courses; and an *à la carte* menu, with a choice of seven or eight first courses, main courses and puddings.

When the Wilsons first went to the Peat Inn seventeen years ago supplies of food were the difficulty we all found them to be in those days. Since then, however, the situation has improved out of all recognition. David buys virtually everything locally. He feels that if you stick to fresh produce, you can't go wrong. Fresh produce means using whatever is in season, and many of his supplies come directly to him – people know that no one else in the area will be interested in, for example, baskets of chanterelles and boletus, so they are brought straight to David. He only buys native breeds of beef, and that from within his area. He usually buys only the fillet, but occasionally he uses the rib.

The Wilsons' relaxed, almost laid-back attitude to life belies their extreme professionalism – you can't help enjoying yourself at the Peat Inn, where there is none of the uncomfortable feeling of awe which sometimes goes hand in hand with such an outstanding reputation for food and wine as the Wilsons have earned. It is an unexpected bonus in this day and age of foody prima donnas to come across such a relaxed establishment, where you eat and drink so well in such comfortable surroundings, and this atmosphere emanates directly from David and Pat Wilson. In 1987 they were awarded a Michelin rosette, and thoroughly deserved it.

A quiet road above the village of Peat Inn.
Neighbouring Lothians still see rural Fife as a foreign place.

AIRDS HOTEL

ERIC AND Betty Allen's Airds Hotel has won renown not only in this country but internationally, and no wonder, because Airds is as near perfection as it is possible to get. One of the hotel guides has described it as being 'homely', which, while obviously well meant, is a totally inappropriate word to describe its situation, decor and atmosphere, all of which are superb. Airds is a long, low white hotel set on the eastern shore of Loch Linnhe in Argyllshire, with spectacular views across to the island of Lismore, and to the hills of Morvern beyond. Airds was once the village inn, and the hotel's beautiful garden is across the tiny road.

Inside, Airds is both elegant and comfortable. There are two drawing-rooms, each with a log fire and furnished with comfortable chairs and sofas. The lovely flower arrangements throughout are done by a neighbour

This magnificent stag's head adorns the wall of one of Airds' comfortable drawing-rooms.

in Port Appin. Across the hall is the long dining-room. This has always been an attractive room, but in the past three years it has been revamped to become positively elegant, without seeming in any way out of place in its idyllic setting. There are low windows all down one side, and the walls, warm, with their creamy beige self-coloured wallpaper, are hung with a variety of attractive flower and butterfly prints. The tables are set far enough apart to allow privacy of conversation, the chairs are very comfortable, and the napery is exquisite. All in all, a perfect setting in which to enjoy Betty Allen's food. The elegant Betty is an inspired cook, and is now assisted by her son Graeme, who has Betty's eye for detail as well as her sense of fun. Graeme trained for two years with the Savoy Group, and then spent a year at the Capital in London, before returning to Airds.

The Allens have been at Airds since 1978. Over the years their menus have evolved, reflecting the way fashions have changed in food and cooking. Betty and I agree that cooking is the term to use in Britain, rather than the grand word cuisine, which is so often used in this country to describe inferior produce masked with sauces. There is nothing inferior about the produce used at Airds, or at any of the hotels described in this book. In their early years the Allens had the same struggle to get decent produce and regular supplies as we all used to have. Now they are in the lucky position of being able to choose their suppliers. Betty and Eric grow a certain amount of their own vegetables, notably their varieties of lettuce, mange-tout and sugar snap peas, and all their own herbs.

The wine list at Airds is remarkable. Eric started to drink wine about twenty years ago, when they were living in Kirkintilloch and they gave refuge to two French teachers who could find nowhere to stay for their year in this country. There started a friendship, with one of the girls in particular, which has lasted ever since – Cécile visits them each July, and they visit her family at their home near Lyons. Cécile's father kept a good cellar, and this was Eric's introduction to wine. Until then, as he says, he drank Lutomer Reisling and Mateus Rosé – which is hard to believe! Ten years ago he got down to the serious business of putting together what he calls a 'proper' list. He spends his winter months researching and composing next year's list, and he spends time each winter in Burgundy, where there is active co-operation between the winemakers and their counterparts in California. Over the years Eric has completed the Higher Certificate Course and the Diploma Course with the Wines and Spirits Education Trust. He feels that because he has access to good wines he ends up drinking good wines, and he has to force himself to stock wines at the lower end of the market.

Airds is a member of the prestigious Châteaux et Relais group – one of only three Scottish members to date. They are also members of the Scottish Tourist Board. They feel that the STB rating system is making a genuine effort to raise standards, but that like every bureaucratic body the STB can't see the wood for the trees, and they have got their priorities wrong. In 1989, out of curiosity, Eric did a survey of all their guests during the month of September, in order to see what had brought them to Airds. It makes interesting reading. 45% were returning guests, 22% were recommended to come by friends, 8% were from Châteaux et Relais, 8% had read about it in the *Egon Ronay Guide*, 6% in the *Good Food Guide*, 5% in the excellent Wendy Arnold guide, *The Historic Hotels of Scotland* (its first year), 5% in magazine and newspaper articles, and 1% in the *Good Hotel Guide*.

Eric and Betty feel that visitors come to Airds for the food, wine, attention and comfort. They do. But they come back again and again for the unique experience of staying in such exquisite surroundings, for the peace and beauty, and to be cosseted by the Allens. Eric and Betty are perfect hosts, and Airds is the sort of hotel which gives Scotland a reputation for food, comfort and service on a par with the best in Europe.

Airds Hotel is situated in the village of Port Appin, between Loch Laich,
an inlet of Loch Linnhe, and Airds Bay on the Lynn of Lorn.

Previous pages: Looking across Loch Linnhe from Port Appin.
Above: The Valvona & Crolla shop at 19 Elm Row, Edinburgh.

THERE IS a long-standing relationship between the Scots and the French, known as the Auld Alliance. Between the Scots and the Italians there is just as strong an alliance, even though the relationship doesn't have a name. In every town or city in Scotland there are Italians living, usually involved in catering in some form, whether running small restaurants or making superb ice-creams. In Edinburgh there is an establishment which is the hub of Italian activity in that city, catering for Italians and for many Italia-philes (like me) from all over Scotland: Valvona & Crolla. It describes itself as being an Italian Warehouse, but others might think of it as a delicatessen. We buy all our spices, olives, oils, vinegars, coffee beans (which I freeze) and delicatessen items such as horse-radish and sun-dried tomatoes at this marvellous shop, where every visit – even queueing – is a positive pleasure and entertainment.

Valvona & Crolla is now run by two brothers, Philip and Victor Contini, with Philip's wife Maria and their father Carlo Contini, who was a policeman in Italy in the early 1950s and who, to perfect his English, came to Edinburgh to stay with his friend Vittorio Crolla. Carlo Contini met Vittorio Crolla's sister Olivia, fell in love with her, married her and stayed on in Edinburgh to help his friend run the Warehouse.

The foundation of the business in the early 1920s stemmed from a familiar story. At the turn of the century Vittorio Crolla's father was one of five children of a shepherd in the Abbruzzi mountains, in the south of Italy. As is the custom both in Italy and in Scotland, the eldest son inherited the small amount of land, and there was nothing for the other four children and their families to live on. There was no alternative to emigration. Another statistic was added to the mass migration of Italians to the United States, the United Kingdom, Germany, and elsewhere during the late nineteenth and early twentieth centuries. Why the majority of Italian immigrant families went into catering remains a mystery, but whatever they did and do, these Italians work very hard; they come from peasant communities, and inherent in their make-up is the realization that if you don't work you don't eat. But this does not account for the cheerfulness and fun with which the people at Valvona & Crolla work so very hard. When I asked Philip about this, he told me that they are Southern Italians, that they have a joy of life which stems in a large part from their being very religious people, and they feel that in life you have to treat fellow human beings as equals. Their aim is to make it easy for the customers to enjoy their shopping – they realize that shopping can be such a tiring drudgery, and that it is becoming increasingly anonymous, so they feel it is very important to be kind, friendly and fun to all their customers, as well as continually to be searching out, and offering a choice of, the best available. He sees Valvona & Crolla as being a catalyst between the producer and the consumer.

They encourage their customers to cook, and from fresh ingredients. Philip points out that for those with little time and for those financially less well off, the Italian way of cooking is a cheap way of eating as well as being nutritious and delicious. They recently sponsored Antonio Carluccio's appearance at the Edinburgh Book Festival, and Philip cites one Jean Macdonald, who came down with a group of Italo-philes from Inverness, by bus, for just two hours to hear Antonio talk about mushrooms and fungi. He says that this is just one example of the nucleus, that exists in every Scottish city, of Scots who are mad about Italy – its food, culture and language. I identify with them entirely!

Philip travels to Italy two or three times a year, always looking for new suppliers of the best. Valvona & Crolla are *the* Italian wine specialists in the UK, and they only stock Italian wines. Philip agrees with Sandy Irvine Robertson (see The Grain and the Grape) that Italian wines are in the ascendent. He says that Italian winemakers are only now beginning to realize the quality of the grapes in their own vineyards, and they are no longer imitating the French wines. They are experimenting with their own grapes. Philip says there is a fantastic range of new wines, all coming from Italy these days. Italy used to be thought of as a cheap wine country, but the winemakers now realize that there is a demand for better wines, and there are now some really smart good quality wines, which are relatively inexpensive. The largest winery in Europe is Sella & Mosca, in north-west Sardinia, where they not only have extensive vineyards of their own, but also buy in grapes from other small growers.

Considering the amount of business done by Valvona & Crolla, their shop is really very small; the queue of customers often stretches out into the street. Inside, the long, narrow premises are very tall. Shelves stretch right up the walls on either side of the shop, with those on the right-hand side packed with wine bottles. Lifting bottles off the top shelves is an operation performed with skill and panache, but it makes my heart stop for a few seconds whenever I watch it. The roof is hung with salamis, bundles of sugared almonds and, at Christmastime, *panettones*. For all the many years that I have shopped there, a hairy wild boar haunch complete with trotter has hung among the other stuff. In fact wild boar fillets are sold at Valvona & Crolla, but the hairy haunch is something of a joke. They sell Italian breads and rolls, made daily and their fresh and dried pasta is made by Cosmo, the famous Italian restaurateur in Edinburgh, who started many years ago with a tiny restaurant in a basement in Broughton Street.

Valvona & Crolla never have any trouble with staff. Philip says that when they need someone, they put a little notice on their door and someone always knows of someone who wants a job. The main qualifications for being employed by Valvona & Crolla are to be outgoing, to have an ability to work in cramped conditions, and always to have a smile!

Bread baked in all shapes and sizes is sold at Valvona & Crolla, where the queues can stretch out into the street.

FRESH FISH

—— AND ——

SHELLFISH

In the cold waters around the coast of Scotland swim
the best fish in the world for eating. Although the
Scots have always eaten fish as part of their staple
diet, they have, until recently, been very conservative
in choosing which fish they eat. For the most part, the
Scottish fish diet has been first and foremost haddock,
then herring and mackerel. When we first started our
hotel lives seventeen years ago the only fish we served
our guests (apart from breakfast-time kippers and
mackerel) was salmon.

*Opposite: Fly-fishing on the River Spey. Above: Fly-fishing
tackle. People will come from all over Europe for the
opportunity to catch salmon, 'the king of fish'.*

I WAS QUITE uneducated myself in those days when it came to fish-eating, and completely unaware of the wonderful fish in the Minch (the stretch of water between Skye and the mainland), right on my doorstep! In those days any fish like monkfish which were caught in the nets were thrown straight back into the sea – it makes me weep to think of it now, when we pay dearly for monkfish. Even then, though, there was much exporting of shellfish to the continent, and these days our narrow roads can be made even more terrifying by an encounter with a huge refrigerated lorry, carrying our precious fish and shellfish to Spain. These lorries run on a regular basis two or three times a week, and there is an even heavier demand for fish in Europe, in Spain particularly, just before a religious festival. On these occasions, the price of fish shoots up, unless, like us, you are very fortunate in having an excellent supplier, who appreciates the fact that our demand for fish is constant, and who pegs his prices. Over and over again I am thankful for our food suppliers, without whom we could not produce the food we do. They are vital to us and the other hotels in this book, and I believe there is a very appreciative mutual respect between us all and our suppliers.

We get our fish from three sources, to ensure a sufficient supply; from George Lawrie in Mallaig, a fourth generation fish smoker, and a good friend as well as a fine fish merchant; Andy Race, also in Mallaig, who telephones us for our order on a Saturday and delivers to our door on a Tuesday; and our third supplier is Duncan Fraser, the fish merchant and game dealer in Inverness. Duncan buys his fish from Buckie, Portsoy and Aberdeen, but chiefly from Kinlochbervie. He says that supplies of fish such as halibut, turbot and monkfish are better from the west than the east coast. He attributes this difference to the feeding grounds – here in the west we have the Gulf Stream, which must encourage a superior feeding ground

Above: A rich harvest of 'Dublin Bay' prawns.
Opposite: Lobsters, crab and other
crustacea all caught from Raasay.

for fish. Duncan Fraser says that fish caught on the east coast just don't seem to have the same shelf life as west coast fish.

All three of our suppliers can obtain shellfish as well as the monkfish, halibut, turbot and hake we buy from them. Probably the shellfish we use more than any other are the huge Dublin Bay prawns – also known as Norwegian lobsters. We get scallops, and in this country we eat the coral crescent-shaped roe as well as the white muscle of the fish. We buy farmed mussels, which are much cleaner, because they grow up ropes instead of clustered around rocks where the sand washes through them. Here on the shore below Kinloch grow huge horse mussels, called Clabach Dubhs (pronounced clappy doos!), which are impossible to eat because they are always full of tiny seed pearls. To bite on one can be agony! We are very lucky to have a regular supply of farmed oysters from Broadford, from the South Skye Oyster Company, and lobsters arrive each week from an enterprising lobster fisherman at Torrin, down the Elgol peninsula.

Salmon is virtually a subject all its own. There are two types of salmon to be had in Scotland – wild, and farmed. We use only wild salmon, because I think it is greatly superior to the farmed variety. Several years ago we began to write the 'wild' as a prefix to salmon when it was on the menu here – the height of pretentiousness, I thought at the time. But now that farmed salmon has become so much more prevalent I wouldn't dream of *not* describing it thus.

We buy our salmon from the Moray Fish Co. in Portree, where the efficient and friendly Catriona Matheson looks after us so well that we feel positively cosseted. She telephones us when they have a catch in, asking how many fish we would like sent down to us. Our salmon arrive with our main fruit and vegetable deliveries by courtesy of Norman Macleod in Portree.

Wild salmon, often called the king of fish, vary throughout their season. The salmon fishing season is from late February to late August, but they are not caught near us until well into April. The earliest-caught salmon I have cooked was caught in mid April, and it was superb, moist and almost gelatinous. Early fish have a bright, silvery colour. This becomes less bright in the months of July and August. There is something almost magical about salmon – partly, I'm sure, because of the way they leap. Cooked, fresh salmon has a creamy substance between each flake, due to the bands of fat throughout the fish. My favourite part of a fish is the tail end.

Like all fish, salmon can easily be ruined in the cooking. It is vital not to overcook. We clean (gut), fillet and skin salmon – this may sound an arduous task, but I assure you it really isn't, providing that you have a really sharp filleting knife. We cut the filleted salmon into pieces about three or four inches long, and put them on a baking tray, with a slice of butter on top of each piece of salmon. They are baked in a hot oven (420°F/200°C/gas 6), for 5 minutes. This method was demonstrated to me by John Tovey, the eminent cook and hotelier and author, from Miller Howe, on Lake Windermere.

To cook a whole fish for serving cold there is one fool-proof method. You do need a fish kettle, but if you don't own one yourself, you may well find that a nearby hotel or restaurant will lend you one – we always do, here at Kinloch! Clean the fish, and put into the fish kettle on the trivet (the metal stand which lifts out). Cover it with cold water, and I add a bottle of dry white wine. To the liquid in the kettle add a couple of handfuls of parsley, a small handful of peppercorns (black or white), two teaspoons of rock salt and several slices of lemon. Over a moderate heat, gradually bring the liquid in the fish kettle to a rolling simmer. As soon as it is at this stage, take the fish kettle off the heat and leave it in a cool place, till the liquid is cold. Then take up the salmon, and skin it and arrange it on a pretty serving plate or ashet. This is foolproof, regardless of the weight of the fish, because the amount of time the water takes to come to the boil varies according to the size of the fish – the bigger the fish, the longer the water takes to come to boiling point, and also the longer it takes to cool. The fish will always be perfectly cooked.

An alternative way to cook a piece of salmon for serving hot is to wrap it in buttered foil, with handfuls of parsley, lemon slices and peppercorns and rock salt. Put the foil parcel in a roasting tin with water coming half-way up the sides of the fish. Bake it thus in a moderate oven, for about 20 minutes per pound.

Often you see salmon steaks for sale in shops. My advice is to avoid these, because they are usually cut too thin. But if you do have some salmon steaks to cook, and want to grill them, cook them under a moderate heat – too high a heat will render them tough on the outside. Baste them regularly under the grill with melted herb butter, and turn them over during cooking time so that they are cooked evenly from each side. A steak about one inch thick will need two or three minutes' cooking each side. Remove the skin by twisting it in the prongs of a fork before serving the salmon steaks.

I have mentioned that I dislike farmed fish. However, there are fish farms and fish farms, and one of the very best is Strathaird Salmon Farms, not far from us at Straithaird, near Elgol. This particular salmon farm is owned by Ian Anderson, better known to some as the singer and composer Jethro Tull, who has earned an international reputation and standing in the history of contemporary music over the years to rival that of the Rolling Stones. Strathaird is extremely well and efficiently run by the manager, Robert Kelly, together with Ian Anderson, who argues defensively in favour of farmed salmon. Ian says that the future of fish farms now lies in quality as opposed to quantity. He explained to me the difference in texture between wild and farmed fish (farmed fish tend to be softer, sometimes almost mushy in texture, compared to the firm texture of wild salmon): once farmed fish are killed they are bled and immediately kept at a temperature of 2°C/36°F, which doesn't allow the bands of fat in the salmon to break down bacterially – really, the difference could be compared to the difference between meat which has been hung and that which hasn't. In 1982 Ian Anderson started a salmon processing plant in Inverness, from where smoked salmon is exported in quantity to the United States as well as to Europe, and also to Harrods. Through his efforts, Ian Anderson contributes in no small way to the Scottish economy.

The other side of fish farming is that the price of farmed salmon has now fallen so low as to be unviable for the smaller enterprises, which fact explains the number of individual fish farms currently on the market. Many of

*A classic painting of salmon fishing in Scotland
from the Pittodrie House Hotel collection.*

the fish farms, though, are owned by huge conglomerates; for example, Marine Harvest is part of the Unilever Group. Yet even these fish farms are not immune from the general economic climate of fish farming. One of the many Marine Harvest fish farms here in Skye recently had to axe a large percentage of its work force, so the argument that fish farms provide a valuable source of employment is looking rather thin, as work in a fish farm can no longer be viewed as permanent. My other reason for hating fish farms is twofold: they are an eye-sore – you can rarely pass a stretch of water in Scotland without its appearance being marred by the unsightly cages of a fish farm; and fish farming is undeniably harmful ecologically. As far as the waters are concerned, the natural balance must be upset by the fish faeces and excess fish food which fall into the waters around the cages. This has

been described to me by one fish farm manager as nutrification of the water, but another word would be pollution. Nuvan, the chemical used to keep sea lice off farmed fish (sea lice are washed off wild fish as they swim up rivers) has a bad press, which may account for the fact that the name Nuvan has recently been changed to Aquagard. Now, I am no chemist, but I believe that this chemical is used in such minute quantities as to be virtually harmless to man. However, it is very noticeable that the rock pools on a beach near us in Skye are devoid of pool life such as sea anemones and shrimps, and this particular beach with the lifeless rock pools is just down the coast from a fish farm. Can it really only be coincidence? From another ecological standpoint, there are forms of wildlife indigenous to these beautiful parts of Scotland which are harmful to farmed fish, and so unscrupulous fish farm workers get rid of them. In 1989 a fish farm manager here in Skye was fined a paltry £200 for shooting twenty herons. Other species also at risk are seals and otters.

For me, the wild fish is preferable by far to the farmed. I am always amazed when I read of cooks and food writers who claim not to be able to tell the difference between the two. Quite apart from the vast difference in cost, they are different in colour, texture and taste.

Of all the flat fish that swim off our shores, the two we use regularly here at Kinloch are halibut and turbot. My favourite is halibut, in fact halibut is one of my two favourite white fish for eating. In London recently I tried to buy some filleted halibut, to be told in amazement that it wasn't stocked because it would cost an exhorbitant £18 a pound weight! We are currently paying between £8 and £9 a pound for halibut.

As with all fish, halibut benefits from being cooked in the simplest way. Not for me combinations of these beautifully flavoured succulent fish with ingredients like raisins, ginger, and fruit. I like to cook my fish with flavours which to me are complementary to the fish itself, and to serve with it a sauce which enhances the natural flavours. To me, the acidity of fruit such as plums, and spices like ginger is too intrusive on the natural flavours of the fish. One of the ways we cook halibut – and turbot, too, which has a slightly slacker and less dense texture than halibut – is to make a fish stock by simmering together water, onions, fish skins and bones, peppercorns, and a handful of parsley, with white wine. After about 30 minutes' simmering we strain this and gently poach the filleted fish in the liquid. You can see when the fish is cooked, the length of time depends on the thickness of the fish, but generally speaking 3–5 minutes of gentle simmering will be sufficient cooking time.

Monkfish is another of my favourites, and this fish we cook in only one way, a method which is simplicity itself and which can also be used for cooking fillets of halibut or turbot – or any other fish for that matter, such as plaice or sole. I butter an ovenproof dish well, and cover the base of the dish with parsley, ground pepper and lemon juice squeezed over. I then lay the pieces of

Fishing boats at Ullapool. This village was built as a herring station in the 1780s but, owing to the scarcity of herring, it now deals mainly in mackerel.

*Previous pages: A fishing boat heading out to sea along Loch Broom.
Above: A magnificent platter of seafood.*

fish or monkfish tails on this, cover with more parsley and squeezed lemon juice, cover the dish with a lid and bake till the fish is cooked. Cooked this way, monkfish tails emerge soft and creamy-textured; if they are poached they tend to shrink and toughen.

Hake is my other favourite white fish. Down south, hake fetches exorbitant prices, but up here in Scotland people are slightly wary of hake, so its price is the same as that of cod. But much as I like eating good fresh cod, hake is superior by far. It is an evil-looking fish, with its long, almost eel-like body, and a positively menacing face and head. I wouldn't blame anyone suddenly experiencing a loss of appetite on seeing a whole hake. We buy them whole usually, and fillet them ourselves, but in a fishmonger's they will look much better ready filleted. They have a firm texture and an almost sweet and nutty taste when very fresh. We dip them in beaten egg and then in pinhead oatmeal, fry them in butter and sunflower oil combined, and serve them with a good tartare sauce – a sauce which has been so abused by the food industry and rendered so revolting that I wonder just how many people bother to make the real thing. It is one of the very best sauces, and is perfect for serving with hake cooked as I've described. We don't serve trout here, unless a guest catches one. Wild trout are delicious, but the farmed trout which can be readily bought are usually very dreary fish, rather muddy in taste.

Herring are sadly becoming a rarity. Herring used to

be known as the silver darlings, and their scarcity is due to overfishing. The word soon goes round when there are good herring available, and they are best cooked dipped in oatmeal and shallow fried.

Mackerel are such rich fish that I only like to eat them at lunchtime; eaten for supper or dinner, they make their presence felt for the rest of the night, in my experience. They are firm and succulent, and can be grilled or baked.

We are very lucky in getting a ready supply of farmed oysters. Oysters used to be such a staple part of the diet in previous centuries. I have read that Edinburgh people used to devour a hundred thousand oysters a day! Native oysters, which these were, are a different breed to the farmed oysters available to us these days. Native oyster supplies have dwindled to near extinction owing to pollution and a variety of diseases and parasites, according to John Noble, who, together with Andrew Lane, is the best-known oyster farmer in Scotland today. They farm oysters on Loch Fyne, and have done so for more than ten years now. These farmed oysters are of the gigas variety, smaller than the native oyster but delicious to eat. We occasionally serve them as a first course, simply fried in butter with pieces of smoked bacon – all fish and shellfish have a peculiar affinity with bacon – and served with a creamy sauce made by swirling cream together with the juices of bacon and oyster in the frying pan. We also use oysters in a sauce for serving with turbot.

As I've already said, we get through a frightening quantity of these wonderful huge Dublin Bay prawns. Whole, they are also known as Norwegian lobsters, but once their heads are removed they can legally be referred to as scampi! Rather confusing. They are, however, almost sweet in flavour, and very filling. They need the briefest time in simmering water, before being scooped out and cooled to the point where they won't burn your fingers as you shell them. They can be painful to shell, as their shells are so hard and sharp. The best way to shell them is to squeeze them lengthways, then press apart their shells either side of the flat middle section. The shell then comes off quite easily, enabling you to pull the cooked prawn out. We use prawns in a number of ways – either chopped in a creamy sauce to serve with halibut, turbot or monkfish, or as a filling for spinach or watercress *roulades*, or in a rich pâté, or in a salad to serve with avocado and tomato terrine, or with a spinach and garlic terrine. Prawns are endlessly useful, and greatly enjoyed by all who can eat shellfish.

Lobster can be terribly disappointing, which is why I never choose lobster in a city restaurant. For a start, you have to understand that lobsters hate travel. They exude an enzyme which impairs their flavour, and they can so easily be rendered tough by overcooking. Small lobsters are much sweeter in taste than great big ones. One of the miracles of nature for me is the transformation from the live lobster, in its handsome dark navy blue shell, to the cooked lobster with its brilliant orangey red shell. To cook lobster, have a pan of boiling water, and plunge the lobster in. It may sound cruel if I say that this is best done while the lobster is still alive, but it is probably preferable to trying to stab it to death, which is the other way of killing them. A lobster weighing a pound or so needs to be boiled for about 15 minutes. Lobsters aren't very plentiful for us here in Skye, and we usually serve them chopped into a creamy sauce with chives, to embellish baked halibut.

We are lucky to have a plentiful supply of marvellous crab. To be honest, I prefer crab to lobster. If you get live crab, you can safely pick them up by holding them between finger and thumb at their back, from top to bottom, without fear of their large front pincers reaching you. Cook them as for lobster, in boiling water for about 15 minutes to the pound weight. When the crab is cool enough to handle, break open the shell by pressing with your thumbs on the back. Carefully scoop out the dark, soft crabmeat from under the rim of the shell. On the underside of the crab there are distinctive white bits with green tips, known repulsively as the dead man's fingers; throw these away. Everything else can be eaten, and don't forget to bash open the front claws, and scoop out the meat from those. The other claws aren't worth bothering about. Crab is very versatile. Best of all I like to serve it cold, the white and dark meats mixed together, accompanied by two good spoonfuls of mayonnaise. I normally use a tomato and garlic, or a lemon and cucumber mayonnaise. Crab also makes wonderful soup, delicious soufflés, and a very good rich tart.

Of the shellfish we use at Kinloch, scallops are my other favourite. They need very little cooking, and I like them best gently fried in butter, and served with any of the sauces I have already mentioned in this chapter, or with gently cooked spring onions and fresh ginger. Scal-lops are delicious wrapped in streaky bacon, pushed on to skewers and barbecued – the bacon prevents the scallop from drying out. Scallops are also delicious in a white wine sauce, served on a bed of rice.

Squid falls into the category of food which people either love or loathe. We feature it on our menus here from time to time because we love it ourselves, and usually there about five other people in the dining-room who feel the same way! Squid needs scrupulously careful preparation, by washing and rinsing, and then pulling on the plastic-like tip of one of the quills; as the quill emerges from inside the squid it will usually bring the insides with it, but if it does an incomplete job, these are easily pulled down with your fingers. Peel the very fine transparent membrane off the squid body, and slice the squid into rounds. Pat them dry with absorbent kitchen paper, and sauté the pieces of squid gently and briefly in extra virgin olive oil together with finely chopped garlic and a generous grinding of black pepper. The squid is cooked when it turns opaque, after between two and four minutes, depending on how much squid there is in the pan. Before serving, dredge with finely chopped parsley and serve with a wedge of lemon at the side. This, for me, is the nicest way of serving squid.

If I had to choose one type of food above all others to eat for the rest of my life, it would be fish, and I often think how lucky we are to have such an abundance of excellent fish at our disposal.

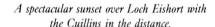

A spectacular sunset over Loch Eishort with the Cuillins in the distance.

Spinach and garlic terrine, a delicious and healthy summer dish.

SPINACH AND GARLIC TERRINE WITH PRAWNS AND TOMATOES

This garlic-flavoured spinach terrine makes a good first course, or an equally good main course for a summer lunch.

Serves 8–10

2lb / 900g frozen spinach, thawed and well drained
1–2 large garlic cloves, peeled and chopped
5oz / 1¼ cups / 150g Cheddar cheese, grated
4 size 2 / US extra large eggs
1 size 2 / US extra large egg yolk
about ½ tsp freshly grated nutmeg
salt and freshly ground black pepper
10 small, ripe tomatoes
1lb / 450g shelled cooked prawns (shrimp)
4 tbsp extra virgin olive oil
2 tbsp balsamic vinegar
few fresh basil leaves

Line the short ends and the bottom of a 2lb / 900g terrine or loaf tin with baking parchment. Put the drained spinach into a food processor together with the chopped garlic and the grated cheese. Whiz to make a smooth purée. Then, still whizzing, add the whole eggs, one by one, and the egg yolk. Add the nutmeg, and salt and pepper to taste.

Pour this mixture into the prepared terrine. Smooth even, and cover the surface with a strip of baking parchment. Put the terrine into a roasting tin and add enough water to come halfway up the sides of the terrine. Bake in a preheated moderate oven (350°F / 180°C / gas 4) for 1½ hours. Remove from the oven and leave to cool completely – ideally overnight.

Skin the tomatoes: dip each in boiling water for a few seconds after which the skin will slip off easily. Cut each tomato in half, then each half in 6 wedges, scooping out the seeds. Mix in a bowl with the prawns (shrimp). Cut any huge prawns (shrimp) in half. Stir in the olive oil, balsamic vinegar, salt and pepper to taste and the torn basil leaves.

Turn out the spinach and garlic terrine on to a serving plate or ashet. Spoon around the tomato and prawn (shrimp) mixture.

BAKED FILLETS OF HALIBUT WITH CREAMY LOBSTER SAUCE

Halibut is one of my favourite white fish – hake is the other – firm fleshed and succulent. This is the simplest way to cook fish, and, I think, the best. The sauce is luxurious!

Serves 6

2oz / 4 tbsp / 60g butter
2 good handfuls of parsley, stalks (stems) and all
juice of 1 lemon
freshly ground black or white pepper
6 pieces of halibut fillet, each weighing about 6oz / 175g

Lobster Sauce

½ pint / 1¼ cups / 300ml single (light) cream
2 oz / 4 tbsp / 60g butter
1 tsp plain (all-purpose) flour
3 egg yolks
salt and freshly ground white pepper
juice of 1 lemon
6–8oz / 175–225g cooked lobster meat, chopped

First make the sauce. Put the cream, butter, flour, egg yolks, and salt and pepper to taste into a liquidizer or food processor and whiz until smooth. Pour this into a heatproof bowl. Put the bowl in a wide pan or roasting tin containing enough gently simmering water to come halfway up the sides of the bowl and place over a low heat. Cook until the sauce thickens, stirring with a wire whisk from time to time. This will take 25–35 minutes.

Meanwhile, thickly butter a wide, shallow ovenproof dish. Lay half of the parsley on the bottom, sprinkle half the lemon juice over, and grind pepper over too. Put the pieces of fish on this bed of parsley, and cover with the remaining parsley. Sprinkle over the remaining lemon juice, and grind more pepper over. Cover the dish with a lid and bake in a preheated moderate oven (350°F / 180°C / gas 4) until the fish is cooked; if you are cooking in a pyrex dish with a pyrex lid this will take 20–30 minutes, depending on the thickness of the fish. If your lid is foil, allow a rather longer cooking time because foil is such a poor conductor of heat.

When the sauce has thickened, keep the bowl of sauce warm but off direct heat. Just before serving, stir in the lemon juice and chopped lobster meat. Serve spooned over each piece of baked halibut.

OYSTERS WITH SMOKED BACON IN CHIVE CREAM SAUCE, WITH CROUTONS

For a first course, I allow about 4 oysters per person and serve on warmed plates, with two croutons at the side of each portion.

Serves 6

2oz / 4 tbsp / 60g butter
1 tbsp sunflower oil
12 smoked back bacon rashers
(slices of Canadian bacon)
24 farmed (cultivated) oysters,
removed from shells
$\frac{1}{4}$ pint / $\frac{2}{3}$ cup / 150ml double (heavy)
cream
pinch of salt
freshly ground white pepper
small bunch of chives, snipped

Croûtons

12 circles or triangles of white bread
butter for frying.

First make the croûtons: fry the pieces of bread in hot butter until golden brown on both sides, then drain and arrange on a baking sheet lined with kitchen paper.

Keep warm in a low oven.

Heat the butter and oil in a wide shallow pan. Snip the bacon into bits about 1 inch / 2·5cm using scissors, and add to the butter and oil. Cook until the bacon just begins to turn golden brown in its fat. Pour the oysters into the pan and cook for a few minutes, stirring the contents of the pan around so that they cook evenly. Pour in the cream, and season with the salt and a generous grinding of pepper. Let the cream and juices bubble for a couple of minutes. Stir in the chives.

HOLLANDAISE SAUCE

This is the perfect sauce to serve with just about any dish, but perhaps more than anything else with salmon. Make sure that there is plenty – nothing is worse than being mean with hollandaise sauce!

Serves 6, generously

6 tbsp white wine vinegar
1 bayleaf
6–8 black peppercorns
$\frac{1}{2}$ onion, peeled and sliced
8oz / 2 sticks / 225g butter, cut into 8
equal bits
4 size 2/ U S extra large egg yolks

Into a small saucepan, put the wine vinegar, bayleaf, peppercorns and onion slices. Simmer gently until the liquid has reduced by half. Strain into a heatproof bowl, and beat in one piece of butter. Then beat in the egg yolks. Put the bowl over a saucepan of simmering water, or into a roasting tin containing simmering water, placed over moderate heat. Beat continuously, gradually adding the remaining pieces of butter. When you have a thick sauce, and all the butter is incorporated, serve as soon as possible.

If your sauce shows the merest sign of splitting (beginning to curdle), spoon a little of the water from the pan in the the sauce, take the sauce off the heat and beat vigorously. This should do the trick and bring the sauce together again.

SCALLOPS SAUTEED WITH FRESH GINGER AND SPRING ONIONS IN CREME FRAICHE

Scallops and crab vie with each other for being my favourite shellfish. Scallops need so little cooking – too much cooking renders them tough and chewy – and in this recipe they are sautéed gently in butter and served in a sauce which complements their exquisite flavour beautifully. I like to serve this dish with boiled basmati rice, and a mixed green salad with a herby dressing. In Britain we eat the roe, the coral crescent at the side of the white meat of the scallop, and I am always surprised at its lack of appearance when eating scallops in the United States. Scallops are very filling, and 4 per person is generous.

Serves 8

32 scallops (sea scallops)
3oz / 6 tbsp / 90g butter
about 12 spring onions (scallions),
trimmed down to about 2 inches / 5cm
of green above the bulb,
then sliced thinly
2 inch / 5cm piece of fresh root ginger,
peeled and finely chopped
freshly ground pepper, preferably white
12oz / $1\frac{1}{2}$ cups / 350g crème fraîche
chopped parsley (optional)

Trim the black bit off the side of each scallop. Melt the butter in a wide shallow pan, add the scallops and sauté in the butter for about 30 seconds on each side. Put them as they cook into a warmed serving dish.

When all the scallops are cooked, put the sliced spring onions (scallions) and ginger into the pan, and cook for 2–3 minutes. Add a good grinding of pepper, then stir in the crème fraîche. Let the sauce bubble for another couple of minutes, then pour it over the scallops in the serving dish, sprinkle with chopped parsley, if you like, and serve.

A selection of George Lawrie's fish.

Barbecued Salmon with Tomato, Garlic and Cucumber Mayonnaise

This is my favourite way of cooking salmon because I think it's the most delicious. You can barbecue the foil-wrapped fish whole, but it does take so much longer to cook that I prefer to fillet the fish first. With barbecued salmon I serve a well-flavoured mayonnaise, with diced tomatoes and cucumber stirred through it. It looks attractive, and is convenient in that the mayonnaise can be made the day before it is to be served, with the addition of the tomatoes and cucumber on the day.

Serves 8

9–10lb / 4–4.5kg salmon, filleted
butter
freshly ground black pepper
lemon juice
several sprigs of parsley

Tomato, garlic and cucumber
mayonnaise

1 size 2 / US extra large egg
1 size 2 / US extra large egg yolk
1 large garlic clove, peeled and chopped
1 tsp sugar
½ tsp salt
1 rounded tsp mustard powder
¾ pint / 2 cups / 450ml sunflower oil
¼ pint / ⅔ cup / 150ml wine vinegar
4 ripe but firm tomatoes, skinned,
seeded and diced
about 4 inch / 10cm piece of cucumber,
peeled, halved lengthways,
seeded and finely diced

To make the mayonnaise, put the egg and yolk into a food processor or liquidizer, together with the chopped garlic, sugar, salt, mustard and plenty of pepper and whiz. Still whizzing, add the oil, a drop at a time until the mayonnaise begins to thicken, then in a steady trickle. Whiz in the wine vinegar. Scrape the mayonnaise into a bowl, cover with clingfilm (plastic wrap) and store in the refrigerator until required.

To barbecue the fish, place each fillet in a large piece of heavy-duty foil. Liberally butter the fish, pepper it, squeeze lemon juice over it and tuck several sprigs of parsley around it. Wrap the foil around the fish to make a parcel and slash the foil in several places in order to let the charcoal flavour permeate through into the fish. Place the parcels on the barbecue once the charcoal has burned down to a white heat and cook the fish for 4–5 minutes on each side.

Stir the diced tomatoes and cucumber into the mayonnaise, and serve with the fish.

Hake Fillets in Oatmeal with Tartare Sauce

Hake is one of my favourite white fish, and very underrated. In its entirety, a hake is a rather fearsome fish to behold, with none of the ugly but appealing look of a monkfish, for example. We buy our hake whole and fillet them ourselves (truly, not such an awful task providing you have extremely sharp knives), but they are bought from fishmongers ready filletted. The hake flesh is close-textured and almost nutty sweet in flavour. Coated with oatmeal and shallow fried till crunchy, it is a filling main course, and I don't usually accompany it with potatoes. A correctly made tartare sauce is perfectly delicious served with it.

Serves 8

2 eggs
8oz / 1⅓ cups / 225g pinhead oatmeal
(coarse Scotch oats)
freshly ground black pepper
8 pieces of hake fillet
sunflower oil for frying

Tartare sauce

1 size 2 / US extra large egg
1 size 2 / US extra large egg yolk
1 tsp sugar
½ tsp salt
1 tsp Dijon mustard
1 garlic clove, peeled and chopped
½ pint / 1¼ cups / 300ml sunflower oil
3 tbsp wine vinegar
2 hard-boiled eggs, shelled and finely
chopped
1 tbsp finely chopped parsley
1 tbsp finely chopped mixed fresh herbs
such as chives, dill, chervil
1 tsp capers, chopped
6 black olives, stoned and chopped

To make the sauce, put the egg and the yolk into a liquidizer or food processor and add the sugar, salt, Dijon mustard, chopped garlic and pepper to taste. Whiz. Still whizzing, gradually add the oil, drop by drop to begin with; then as the mayonnaise sauce thickens, add the oil in a thin trickle. Whiz in the vinegar. Scrape the sauce into a bowl, and fold in the chopped hard-boiled eggs, parsley and other herbs, capers and olives. Cover the bowl and store in the refrigerator until required.

In a wide, shallow dish beat the eggs. In another shallow dish, put the oatmeal and mix black pepper to taste into the oatmeal. Dip each piece of fish first in beaten egg then in seasoned oatmeal.

Heat the oil in a frying pan and fry the pieces of coated fish, in batches, for 2 or 3 minutes on each side, removing them as they are cooked to a dish lined with several thicknesses of kitchen paper. Keep warm in a low oven until all are cooked.

Serve the fish hot, with the sauce.

CREAMY CRAB TART

This is a rich dish, and needs only a good green salad to accompany it. As well as being a good main course dish, it makes an excellent first course. I like to use half white crabmeat and half brown.

Serves 8

Pastry

4oz / 1 stick / 120g butter, hard from the refrigerator
6oz / 1¼ cups / 175g plain (all-purpose) flour
2 tsp icing (confectioners') sugar
½ tsp salt

Filling

2 size 2 / US extra large eggs
2 size 2 / US extra large egg yolks
¼ pint / ⅔ cup / 150ml single (light) cream
good dash of Tabasco sauce
freshly grated nutmeg
freshly ground black or white pepper
1lb / 450g crabmeat
1 tbsp snipped chives

For the pastry, cut the butter into the food processor and add the other ingredients. Whiz until the mixture resembles bread-crumbs, then pat it over the bottom and sides of a flan or quiche dish about 9 inches / 23cm in diameter. Put the dish into the refrigerator to chill for at least half an hour, or more if possible. Then put the pastry case straight into a preheated moderate oven (350°F / 180°C / gas 4) and bake for 20–25 minutes, until the pastry is golden brown. Take it out of the oven and allow to cool.

To make the filling, beat together the eggs, yolks, cream, Tabasco, a little nutmeg, and pepper to taste. Stir this and the crabmeat and chives together well, and pour into the baked pastry case. Return to

the moderate oven and bake for about 20 minutes, until the filling is just firm to the touch. Let the tart sit for 20 minutes before cutting.

BAKED MONKFISH TAILS WITH SORREL AND LIME SAUCE

Monkfish tails vary so much in size that there is no point my saying allow two tails per person. But for 6 people I would allow about 2lb / 900g monkfish tails. Baked as they are in this recipe, the monkfish will be creamy soft, with none of the shrinkage that occurs when the tails are poached, and no hint of toughness.

Serves 6

2oz / 4 tbsp / 60g butter
2 good handfuls of parsley, stalks (stems) and all
freshly ground black pepper
lemon juice
2lb / 900g monkfish tails

Sauce

½ pint / 1¼ cups / 300ml single (light) cream
2oz / 4tbsp / 60g butter
3 size 2 / US extra large egg yolks
1 tsp plain (all-purpose) flour
grated rind and juice of 2 limes
pinch of salt
freshly ground white pepper
handful of sorrel

First make the sauce. Into a liquidizer, put the cream, butter, egg yolks, flour, lime rind, salt, and pepper to taste. Whiz until smoothly blended together, then pour into a heatproof bowl. Put the bowl in a wide saucepan of simmering water, with the water coming one-third to halfway up the sides of the bowl. Place over moderate heat and cook until the sauce thickens – about 20–25 minutes. Stir the contents of the bowl from time to time with a wire whisk. Meanwhile, liquidize the sorrel leaves with the lime juice.

While the sauce is cooking, bake the fish. Butter an ovenproof dish, and cover the bottom of the dish with half of the parsley, freshly ground black pepper and a good squeeze of lemon juice. Lay the monkfish tails over this, and cover them with more parsley, pepper and lemon juice. Put a lid on the dish and bake the fish in a preheated moderate oven (350°F / 180°C / gas 4) for about 25 minutes, or longer if the dish is covered with foil as foil is such a poor conductor of heat.

When the sauce is thick, stir in the sorrel purée. If necessary, keep the sauce warm in the pan of water off the heat. Spoon over the fish and serve.

A sporting print from Ardsheal House.

SMOKING

—— AND ——

SMOKED SPECIALITIES

Smoking, along with salting and drying, has been used as a form of preservation from time immemorial. The Scots are past masters at all three arts, but of all of them it is smoking which produces far and away the most delicious flavour. Smoking used to be associated with fish, but now a wide variety of foods are being smoked by enterprising smokehouses throughout Scotland.

Opposite: Dramatic sunset over Loch Linnhe from Ardsheal House.
Above: The Smokehouse at Mallaig where George Lawrie's
family have been smoking fish for generations.

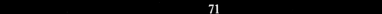

THERE ARE two methods of smoking, cold smoking and hot smoking, and smoking of both sorts takes place usually over oak sawdust, occasionally over a combination of oak and peat. Let's look first at smoking fish.

Cold smoking smokes the fish without cooking it. Some cold-smoked fish, such as salmon, are eaten raw. Others, for example kippers, which are smoked herring, can be eaten raw or cooked. Although kippers are usually thought of as breakfast food, cooked by gentle grilling or by the method I prefer, which is gentle poaching in a frying pan of barely simmering water, they are also delicious filleted and sliced in fine strips, which are marinated overnight in an olive oil, lime juice and onion marinade. This dish is very good served as a first course, accompanied by brown bread and butter, or as a salad main course. There are few things to beat really good kippers – I would far prefer to eat a good kipper than the finest caviar (Godfrey, while loving kippers, wouldn't agree), but finding a good kipper these days is becoming increasingly difficult. Herring are at their best for kippering when they are large fish, resulting in plump kippers. Because of overfishing, however, they are only at their best for a very short time. To kipper herring, the fish are split open and cleaned then dipped in a 90%-salt solution brine for twenty minutes. They are then hung by their heads in pairs and cold smoked overnight. Some dubious fish smokers still dye their kippers a rich shade of mahogany. Dyed kippers are easily spotted, this colour being distinct from the natural pale golden hue of undyed kippers. George Lawrie, the Mallaig fish merchant and smoker, smokes wonderful kippers. George is the fourth generation fish smoker in his family, and seven years ago he was invited to Peru to teach them how to smoke the trout they are farming there. Fish smoking traditionally takes place in a smokehouse, but there are now vast smoking machines as well. George uses both

Above: A selection of smoked products available from Keith Dunbar (opposite, top) at The Summer Isles Smokehouse, Achiltibuie (opposite, bottom).

methods, and he gets equally good results from both, because he knows the quality he is aiming for. At the Summer Isles Foods smokehouse in Achiltibuie, run and owned by Keith Dunbar, there is a Kipper Club, members of which receive two pairs of fresh kippers each month for a year's membership.

Other examples of cold-smoked fish are whiting and Finnan haddock. Finnan haddock get their name from the village of Findon, about six miles down the coast from Aberdeen, where they first smoked haddock, on the bone, to the pale-coloured, delicately smoked fish they should be. They are much nicer on the bone than filleted. Before being cold smoked, the haddock are split, beheaded and cleaned, then briefly dipped in brine – haddock need much less time in the brine than herring, because they are so much less rich in oil. To cook Finnan haddock, poach them gently in milk and serve them with a piece of butter on top. Smoked haddock makes the perfect breakfast, especially when served with poached or scrambled eggs, and it also makes one of the best soups in Scotland. One word of caution while on the subject of smoked haddock: beware the beastly bright yellow fillets of smoked haddock; these have been dyed to this brilliant and unnatural hue, using heaven knows what chemicals, and should be avoided at all costs. Smoked haddock should be pale and golden.

Smoked salmon is a very wide subject these days, thanks to salmon farming. The trouble with smoked salmon is that it is no longer the special-occasion food it once was, and I am afraid that, as with the difference between battery-reared and free-range chickens, people will forget what smoked salmon should be like. It should be pink in colour and soft in texture, not garish orange and rubbery, as it so often is. Wild salmon produces the Rolls-Royce of smoked salmon, but whether the salmon is farmed or wild, Scottish fish are superior to the

*The Maran chickens at Ardsheal House produce
eggs with a unique colour and flavour.*

Norwegian or Pacific fish sometimes used by fish smokers. The Scottish Salmon Smokers Association now have a quality mark which is stamped on packets of smoked salmon to guarantee that the salmon is Scottish and smoked in Scotland, giving that firm, lean smoked fish with an almost satiny texture. Each traditional smoker has his own method of curing salmon; George Lawrie, in Mallaig, uses a combination of salt, demerara sugar, rum and olive oil to coat the sides of salmon, leaving them for about twenty hours before wiping off the coating and smoking the sides of salmon overnight. Keith Dunbar, of Summer Isles Foods at Achiltibuie, uses wild salmon, which he gets from the netting stations at Achiltibuie, and he also uses farmed salmon, which he buys from Shetland. Keith says that he buys his farmed fish only from Shetland because he thinks they are the only people who really know how to use the feed and natural colouring, astrazanthin, which is manufactured by Roche in Switzerland.

Smoked salmon is traditionally served in slices so thin that they are almost transparent, with lemon wedges and brown bread and butter, and freshly ground black pepper. Beware of using too much lemon juice – you only need a squeeze. I love the Jewish combination of cream cheese and smoked salmon with brown bread. But I personally don't like the additions of capers and chopped raw onions served with smoked salmon – both have flavours too strong and overpowering for the delicate

flavour of good smoked salmon. The ends and trimmings can be made into pâté, mousses or terrine.

Hot-smoked fish are smoked at a higher temperature, which means they are cooked at the same time as being smoked. Examples of hot-smoked fish include mackerel, trout, eel and Arbroath Smokies. Some smoked fish, buckling for example, are both cold and hot smoked; buckling are herring which have been cleaned, then hung by their heads and cold smoked for a couple of hours to dry their skins, then hot smoked. They are succulent and delicious. So is smoked trout, served simply with a lemon wedge and buttered brown bread as with smoked salmon, buckling, and smoked eel. The flavour of smoked trout is also nicely complemented by horseradish, and a tablespoon of horseradish stirred into some whipped cream with a squeeze of lemon juice makes a good dressing.

Smoked mackerel is also delicious, but very filling. Enterprising fish smokers are smoking mackerel with a variety of coatings, of which my favourite is crushed black peppercorns. Smoked mackerel needs the accompaniment of lemon juice, to cut through its richness.

Arbroath Smokies are haddock which have been cleaned but left in the round, not split open. They are smoked till their skins are fairly dark in colour, and are good made into pâté, or cooked in simmering milk and served with a piece of butter inside. Inside their dark skins they are a pale golden colour.

Several years ago, when I was writing a book of fish recipes, I was fascinated to discover that a red herring is not just a proverbial saying; it really exists, although it cannot be described as a gastronomic treat. Red herring are made from herring which have spawned. The fish have a slit cut in their necks, but they are left ungutted. They are salted in a barrel for seven days, soaked in fresh water overnight, then hung at the top of the smokehouse for a month. I have never tasted red herring, but I should think you would need to be a devotee of salty/smoky tastes to enjoy it!

Summer Isles Foods at Achiltibuie sell a wide variety of smoked foods as well as smoked salmon and kippers. The smokehouse at Achiltibuie was started in 1977 by Keith Dunbar and Robert Irvine of the Summer Isles Hotel. They were in partnership for five years, then parted amicably, Keith to continue to run the smokehouse, Robert Irvine to concentrate on the hotel and his hydroponicum (an environment for growing plants without soil), where he cultivates fruit and vegetables out of season all year round. In 1977 they only smoked salmon, then they began smoking chickens and poultry produce (such as chicken legs and breasts, and turkey breasts). Now their range includes smoked duck breasts, smoked quail, smoked scallops, prawns and mussels, smoked venison, and venison sausages and cheeses. At first they only supplied local hotels, but now they supply Harrods and the duty-free shops at Heathrow Airport, and Summer Isles Foods employ about twelve people.

The drawback to smoked meats and shellfish is that smoking is a drying process, and the results can be too dry. Clever smokers have devised ways to overcome this problem. At the Rannoch Smokery, owned and run by Leo and Sarah Barclay at Kinloch Rannoch, they use only the best cuts of wild (as opposed to farmed) red deer, the cuts from which are smoked over whisky-impregnated oak. They sell sealed packs of sliced smoked venison with olive oil and herbs, and very good it is, too. They also now make and sell a really good Smoked Venison Pâté, made with cream, butter, red wine, spices and garlic.

Michael and Sue Gibson, the farmers and butchers from Forres, are experimenting with smoked beef. They use the silverside and topside, and to overcome the dryness problem they marinate the meat first. The sample I tried was delicious. They also make sausages from smoked venison, smoked for them by the Pirie smokehouse at Nairn, who do all their smoking. They smoke pheasants, mallard and venison as well, mostly to order for local hotels and restaurants. Smoked venison and beef, sliced thinly, are excellent served with melon, or pears, or with Cumberland Jelly, or Port and Grape Jelly – the sweetness of the fruit or jellies complements the smoky flavours beautifully.

A dramatic contrast of sun and cloud reflected in the water by Rannoch Moor.

Smoked salmon terrine with dill and cucumber at Kinloch Lodge.

SMOKED SALMON TERRINE WITH DILL AND CUCUMBER DRESSING

This is an elegant first course, convenient too, in that it has to be made in advance. It looks most decorative with the creamy and green-flecked sauce.

Serves 8–10

Sufficient sliced smoked salmon to line a terrine or loaf tin
1lb / 450g smoked salmon –
the trimmings and ends are ideal
for this recipe

juice of 1 lemon
4 tbsp cold water
1½ sachets / US 3 envelopes unflavoured gelatine powder (about ¾oz / 22g)
½ pint / 1¼ cups / 300ml milk
dash of Tabasco sauce
freshly ground black pepper
3oz / 90g cream cheese, such as Philadelphia (low fat will do)
½ pint / 1¼ cups / 300ml double (heavy) cream, whipped
1 size 2 / US extra large egg white

Dill and cucumber dressing

handful of fresh dillweed, chopped

½ cucumber, peeled, halved lengthways, seeded and finely diced
¼ pint / ⅔ cup / 150ml thick Greek-style yoghurt

Use the slices of smoked salmon to line an 8–10 inch / 20–25cm long terrine or loaf tin. Put the rest of the smoked salmon into a food processor.

Measure the lemon juice and water into a small saucepan and sprinkle over the gelatine. Let it soak for a minute, then heat gently to dissolve the gelatine completely. Don't let it boil. Take the pan off the heat and cool for a few moments.

Turn on the food processor and whiz

the smoked salmon, then gradually pour in the gelatine liquid. Continue whizzing, and gradually pour in the milk. Season with the Tabasco and black pepper to taste and add the cream cheese. Whiz until all is smooth. Pour this mixture into a bowl, and fold in the whipped cream. Whisk the egg white until very stiff and, using a large metal spoon, fold it into the smoked salmon mixture quickly and thoroughly.

Pour into the lined terrine or tin, cover with clingfilm (plastic wrap) and put in the refrigerator for several hours – or overnight.

To serve, dip the tin into hot water for a few seconds, then unmould on to a serving plate and cut in slices about $\frac{1}{2}$ inch / 1cm thick. For the dressing, just fold together the chopped dillweed, diced cucumber and yoghurt. Serve a spoonful of dressing beside each slice of terrine.

SMOKED TROUT AND HORSERADISH MOUSSE

This is a rich first course. I like to make it in ramekins and unmould each on to a serving plate. Serve with brown toast or bread to accompany the mousse.

Serves 8

3 smoked trout
$\frac{1}{2}$ pint / $1\frac{1}{4}$ cups / 300ml single (light) cream
4 tbsp lemon juice
2 tbsp cold water
1 sachet / US 2 envelopes unflavoured gelatine powder ($\frac{1}{2}$oz / 15g)
4 tsp grated horseradish (not horseradish sauce)
freshly ground black pepper
$\frac{1}{2}$ pint / $1\frac{1}{4}$ cups / 300ml double (heavy) cream, whipped
2 size 2 / US extra large egg whites
2 tbsp chopped parsley

Flake the fish from the smoked trout, removing all bones and skin. Put the flaked fish into a food processor. Whiz, adding the single (light) cream, until you have a

smooth purée. Measure the lemon juice and cold water into a small saucepan and sprinkle the gelatine over the liquid. Let it soak, then heat gently to dissolve the gelatine in the liquid, taking care not to let the liquid boil. Cool for several minutes, then, with the food processor turned on, pour into the smoked trout and cream mixture. (If you pour it in straight from the heat, the mixture tends to curdle.) Add the horseradish and pepper to taste and whiz to blend it in. Add the whipped cream. Turn the mixture into a bowl.

Whisk the egg whites until they are stiff. Using a large metal spoon, fold the whites and parsley quickly and thoroughly through the mousse.

Grease 8 ramekins with a mild oil and divide the mixture evenly between them. Cover and leave in the refrigerator for several hours to set. Dip each ramekin in very hot water for a few seconds to unmould.

SMOKED FISH PATE

You can use any smoked fish for this pâté – smoked salmon, smoked trout, Arbroath smokies, or kippers (smoked and cured herrings). It is a delicious pâté, served with brown toast, or it can be used as a filling for buns or rolls for an up-market picnic.

Serves 6–8

4 kippers, or 3 smoked trout, or 12oz / 350g smoked salmon, or 3 Arbroath smokies
2oz / 4 tbsp / 60g butter
6oz / 175g cream cheese, such as Philadelphia
freshly ground black pepper
juice of 1 lemon

If you are using kippers, first poach them in a shallow pan of water for 5 minutes; drain well. If you are using kippers, Arbroath smokies or smoked trout, flake the fish, removing all skin and bones. Put the flaked fish – or chopped smoked salmon – into a food processor.

Melt the butter over a low heat, then set the pan aside to cool slightly. Whiz the fish in the food processor, slowly adding the melted butter – if you add the butter when it is too hot, the mixture tends to curdle. Add the cream cheese and pepper to taste and whiz until all is smooth. Still whizzing, slowly pour in the lemon juice.

Scrape the pâté into a serving dish and keep, covered, in the refrigerator until required.

Fresh eggs from Ardsheal House.

SMOKED HADDOCK FISHCAKES

Fishcakes are delicious, provided that they are made with fish that tastes. Nothing is as dreary as a fishcake made with haddock (unsmoked), which cries out for tomato ketchup to give it some flavour. Salmon fishcakes, whilst sounding ritzy, so often fall into the tasteless trap, too, but fishcakes made with smoked haddock are REALLY GOOD! They are convenient, too, in that a batch of fishcakes can be made and frozen. If at all possible, use finnan haddock, that is, smoked haddock on the bone.

Serves 8

2lb / 900g smoked haddock
(finnan haddie)
2 pints / 5 cups / 1·25 litres milk
1 onion, peeled and halved
12 medium-sized potatoes,
peeled and halved
4oz / 1 stick / 120g butter
freshly ground black pepper
2 tbsp finely chopped parsley
fresh white or brown breadcrumbs,
toasted
sunflower oil for frying

Put the fish into a pan with the milk and halved onion. Cover with a lid and bring the liquid to simmering point, then cook gently for 3–5 minutes. Take the pan off the heat and let the fish cool in the milk until it is cool enough to handle without pain. Strain off and reserve $\frac{1}{2}$ pint / $1\frac{1}{4}$ cups / 300ml of the milk for mashing into the potatoes. Drain the fish and flake it, carefully picking out all the bones and skin. Set aside.

Cook the potatoes in boiling water until tender, then drain well and mash with the reserved milk and 3oz / 6 tbsp / 90g of the butter. Season with plenty of pepper.

Opposite: A towerhouse near Clatt, Grampian. Below: A sporran worn by Eric Allen of Airds.

Mash the flaked fish and the chopped parsley into the mashed potatoes, and leave until completely cold. Then flour your hands and form the mixture into balls. Flatten the balls and press into the toasted breadcrumbs to coat evenly on each side.

To cook, shallow fry in a small amount of sunflower oil with the remaining butter added, until golden brown on each side. Serve hot.

KIPPER FILLETS MARINADED IN OLIVE OIL AND LIME JUICE

This dish has to be made a day in advance of being eaten.

Serves 8
$\frac{1}{2}$ pint / $1\frac{1}{4}$ cups / 300ml virgin olive oil
1 large mild onion,
peeled and very thinly sliced
juice of 3 limes

8 fresh kipper fillets
(smoked and cured herrings),
each sliced into thin strips lengthways
freshly ground black pepper

Measure the olive oil into a saucepan and add the onion slices. Pour in the lime juice, and heat over a moderate heat until the liquid simmers. Simmer gently for about 3 minutes, then set aside to cool completely.

When cold, pour the lime mixture over the strips of kipper fillets in a serving dish. Grind black pepper generously over all, and cover the dish with clingfilm (plastic wrap). Leave in a cool place for at least 24 hours before serving.

CREAMY SMOKED HADDOCK SOUP

This is my version of a traditional Scottish soup called Cullen Skink, made from smoked haddock and potato. It makes a very good first course and, served in greater quantities, is an equally good lunch or supper dish. It is one of our children's favourites.

Serves 8

2lb / 900g smoked haddock
(finnan haddie),
preferably undyed and,
if possible, smoked
on the bone
1 pint / $2\frac{1}{2}$ cups / 600ml each
milk and water
1 onion, peeled
1 blade of mace
3oz / 6 tbsp / 90g butter
2 onions, peeled and chopped
3 potatoes, or 2 if they are large, peeled
and chopped
freshly ground black or white pepper
freshly grated nutmeg
2 tomatoes, skinned, seeded and
chopped
2 tbsp finely chopped parsley

Put the fish into a saucepan together with the milk and water, the peeled onion and the mace, and put the pan over a moderate heat. Bring the liquid to a gentle simmer and simmer for 3–5 minutes, then draw the pan off the heat and let the fish cool in the liquid until it is cool enough to handle. Strain off the cooking liquid into a bowl and keep – it forms the liquid content of the soup. Flake the fish, removing all skin and bones, and set aside.

Melt the butter in a large saucepan, add the chopped onions and cook until the onions are soft and translucent. Add the chopped potatoes and cook for a further 5 minutes, then pour in the fish cooking liquid. Half cover the pan with a lid and simmer very gently until the pieces of potato are soft.

Liquidize the soup. Rinse out the saucepan, and put the liquidized soup into the clean pan. Season with pepper and nutmeg to taste and stir in the flaked fish and chopped tomatoes. Reheat to serve. Just before serving, stir the parsley through the soup.

BEEF, LAMB

—— AND ——

PORK

Scottish meat is the best in the world.
The only qualification I would make to that statement
applies to the beef, which is certainly the best *if* it
comes from native breeds and is homebred.
We are now getting ever increasing numbers
of beef cattle from continental breeds, such as
Charolais, Limousin and Simmenthal. These give
good beef, but reach a killing weight before their
meat has reached the quality which
comes through maturing.

*Opposite: A typical Borders landscape – dry stone walls,
undulating hills and heather. Above: cattle on the
beach at Skye.*

THE HOMEBRED native breeds, such as Aberdeen Angus, Highland, Shorthorn, Longhorn and Galloway, mature slowly and yield beef of the highest quality.

The differences lies in the method of raising beef cattle. On the one hand, cattle raised for the lower end of the price market are killed between the ages of 11 and 14 months. They are fed up to twenty pounds of grain per animal per day, and the hanging time is minimal. This is because hanging, which is vital for meat to reach good flavour and tenderness, also results in weight loss, so every day that beef is hung means that there is less weight of beef to sell. The resulting beef is a bright, almost pinky red colour, with white-ish fat (the result of a high grain diet), a slightly mushy texture and poor flavour. On the other hand, homebred native beef cattle are relatively slow to mature, reaching their killing weight at about 24 months. They are fed a maximum of four pounds of grain per animal per day, the rest of their feed being made up of natural foodstuffs, such as sugarbeet pulp. They are grazed in fields, and apart from being wormed they are not treated medicinally unless they are ill. By this I mean that they are not injected with antibiotics as a preventative, nor are they given extra hormones or probiotics. After killing, the hindquarters are hung for about 17 days. The beef has a creamy yellow fat (the colour of fat from grass-fed cat-

Above: Note the marbling of fat through this rib of Highland beef, ensuring succulent and tender meat. Opposite: the Grampian mountains near Tyndhum.

tle) and the meat is a dark, plummy red, marbled with fat, which melts during cooking – a kind of self-basting which guarantees tender meat. Such beef is more expensive, obviously, than the other type, but I would far rather eat beef less often and eat better when I do.

Michael Gibson is a farmer as well as a butcher. He lives and farms at Dallas, in Morayshire, providing about half the beef sold at his butcher's shop, called (appropriately) Macbeths, in nearby Forres. Of the other beef sold at Macbeth's, about half is from Orkney, and half from farms to which Mike Gibson sends calves to mature.

Local suppliers will ring him if they have a good Aberdeen Angus, for example, knowing that he only deals in the top end of the market beef. Macbeth's are shortly moving into purpose-built premises, suitable for the ever-increasing amount of work they handle. In addition to butchering and dispatching beef, either by mail-order or by other means, to hotels like ours, as well as to numerous hotels nearer to Forres and many renowned hotels and restaurants in England, they also smoke and make up haggis, black pudding and white pudding. Willie Allen, Mike Gibson's butcher, makes the best black pudding to be found in Scotland, if not in Britain. (Black pudding is a great northern England delicacy as well as a Scottish one.) So often black pudding can be very fatty; Macbeth's black pudding avoids this, and therefore makes a delicious supper dish as well as a breakfast dish. I like to eat it with dry-fried rings of cored apples, while Godfrey prefers it with scrambled eggs and bacon. In their black puddings, white puddings and haggis, they use only stone-ground organic oatmeal, which is so good they also sell it in pound packs in the three varieties: smooth, medium and pinhead. They make several other types of sausage as well as black pudding – Cumberland sausage, herb sausages, a combination of beef and pork sausage, and pork sausages made with no additives or preservatives. They also make venison sausages, and smoked venison sausages, into which they put whichever fruit happens to be in season, usually berries, such as black or red currants or brambles. To compensate for venison's lack of fat, which is so necessary for a good sausage, they use pork fat.

When someone says Scottish beef, the two cuts that spring to most people's minds are the rib roast and the fillet. This is a pity, because there are many other bits of the animal which can be turned into wonderful dishes. My favourite of all beef dishes is a good oxtail stew. Now,

Mike and Sue Gibson with their herd of Highland cattle near Forres. Their cattle are carefully fed and naturally matured.

oxtails don't freeze well raw; I can always detect an oxtail which has been frozen – somehow the flavour and texture are just not the same as with a fresh oxtail. Why this should be so I don't know, because every other bit of beef freezes extremely well. However, when made up into a casserole, the finished dish freezes beautifully. Oxtail casserole must be one of the richest and most satisfying of all winter dishes.

Minced beef is probably the most versatile meat cut (if you can call it a cut) that there is. There are any number of dishes to be made from minced beef, but here a word of warning is in order: buy minced beef only from a quality butcher (like Macbeth's) where you can be sure of buying real minced beef, and not minced bits of the animal which you wouldn't normally contemplate eating. Also, if the minced beef for sale is a very pinky red, this means that there is a high fat content, so look for mince that's a dark plummy red flecked with creamy white. One of our favourite dishes using minced beef is lasagne, made with a meat sauce including bacon, chicken livers, wine, tomato purée and garlic which, if correctly made, transforms lasagne from the bastardized dish it has become in this country to what it should really be like. And it is one of the very best dishes for convenience, too, since it can be frozen successfully, and is one of those dishes which needs to be accompanied only by a good salad. Another favourite recipe which I often use is for meat balls – small, slightly spiced meat balls, which I

serve in a good tomato sauce. They are only as good as the beef with which they are made, but if the beef is good, they make an excellent dish.

Brisket is delicious; it comes from the breast of the animal, and is rather fatty, but slowly cooked with plenty of vegetables, and served either hot or cold, it makes a good dish. Topside and silverside are both cuts which I use for pot-roasting, although topside from a good butcher's can also be roasted. Potroasts are like casseroles; they benefit from cooking, cooling and reheating; somehow the flavours are much improved by cooking twice. This also makes them convenient dishes. Silverside is also good boiled, with whole (peeled) onions, carrots and parsnips, and served with horseradish cream.

How long you roast beef depends on how rare you like to eat it. Between 10 and 15 minutes per pound at a high temperature is about right for most people, plus an extra 10 minutes.

Scottish lamb is as good as the beef. I'm sure that the word lamb in Scotland conjures up the image of the numerous black-faced sheep which you see scattered over the Scottish hillsides – and which, in our part of Scotland, potter all over the place, making driving on our single-track roads even more hazardous. The dimmer animals cross the road just around a corner, thereby making the hapless driver slam on the brakes. Some of the best lamb comes from black-faced sheep crossed with either Suffolks or with Cheviots.

Much of Macbeth's meat is supplied by The Gibson's own farms where they have prize-winning herds of cattle.

Technically the meat can only be called lamb if it is killed within its first year; after that it is called hogget, then it becomes mutton. Our lamb is killed towards the end of its first year and in my opinion it develops more flavour with maturity. Lamb should be hung for anything from seven to ten days – not as long as beef.

How long you roast lamb depends on how well or rare you like your meat cooked. Personally, I find the current vogue for very underdone meat repulsive. The only meat that I like to eat rare is beef, and that I like cooked till the middle is pinky red in colour. Roast leg of lamb for my taste should be barely pink, and a leg weighing about eight pounds needs 15–20 minutes' cooking per pound, in a hot oven. The leg of lamb is also known as the gigot, a Scots word as well as French, just one example of several Scots words which have come down from the Auld Alliance. (Another example is the word ashet, derived from *assiette*. In Scotland an ashet is a serving plate – the sort of plate on which to serve the roast gigot of lamb!) You can buy your lamb on or off the bone, but for me there is no comparison, and we buy all our meat, whether it is lamb, beef or pork, on the bone. I think that much of the flavour comes from the bone, and is lost if your meat is boned. A leg of lamb is also very good served boiled (with vegetables packed around the joint in the casserole dish or saucepan) and accompanied by boiled onions and caper sauce. The stock and vegetables, once cooled and skimmed of fat, make a wonder-

A flock of Michael Gibson's black-faced ewes, the most often-seen sheep in the highlands.

ful soup, thickened with a couple of handfuls of barley.

Another cut of lamb which is delicious roast is the shoulder; the meat from a shoulder of lamb is almost sweet – quite different from the leg. There is much more fat on the shoulder, and a roast shoulder is quite tricky to carve, but for four or five people it makes a delicious roast alternative to the leg. Some people rave about the breast of lamb, but it is altogether too fatty for my taste, and having once stuffed and roasted a breast of lamb I vowed to save myself the bother in the future. Racks of lamb, from the best end of neck, are very good roast, and we serve them with a minty (using applemint) hollandaise sauce. (For a recipe for hollandaise, see the fish chapter. Just add a handful of finely chopped applemint leaves to the sauce.)

Lamb makes wonderful stews and casseroles, combining well with fruit and spices, and also with tomato, herbs and garlic. One of the best stews is Lamb Hotpot, made from either the middle neck or any stewing cut of lamb. The meat is packed into a casserole with layers of sliced onions, potatoes, carrots and cubes of black pudding. You pour water in until it reaches almost to the top of the layer of potatoes which finishes off this dish, which then cooks very long and slowly, is cooled completely and skimmed of any fat, and reheated to serve. It freezes very well.

I have very recently been contacted by two people who are farming kid for the table. I haven't tried it yet

Farmers scrutinizing livestock in the ring at the Inverness sheep auction.

myself, but I am assured that it is delicious, and I feel that I will treat it in the same way as lamb, combining it with either spices and fruit, such as apricots or sultanas, or with olive oil, garlic and tomatoes.

Pork, a most delicious meat providing that it is reared either organically or at least free-range, is one of my favourite meats. Sadly, as with battery chickens, a great number of people have forgotten what 'real' pork tastes like, having grown accustomed to the awful watery stuff which is produced commercially. Equally depressing is the bacon which is for sale in most supermarkets and food shops, bacon which weeps a curd-like substance as it grills, and which shrivels and shrinks before your eyes, and which often tastes of the fishmeal fed to the poor pigs. But good pork and bacon is available in Scotland, as long as you are prepared to ask around or go and look for it! Macbeth's the butchers in Forres buy their pork from a farm outside Huntly, where the pigs are not intensively farmed. They aren't actually free-range, but give very good meat. Pork is hung for about a week – no longer, or the meat will turn sour. The bacon from Macbeth's, both Ayrshire and smoked, is untreated with polyphosphates or water – the polyphosphates hold the water into the bacon, and give bacon that blueish, shot-silk tinge. There is a pig farm in Fife, the only one (so far) in Scotland, which provides naturally raised free-range pork. Near Strathmiglo (although they are due to move nearer to Dundee in the future), the Glentarkie Bacon Company produces pork as it should be and so rarely is. To eat pork from Glentarkie is a treat, and spoils you for eating any other sort. As with beef from homebred native breeds, at Glentarkie the pigs are kept outside in large fields – never more than a hundred pigs to an acre. Their diet is based entirely on natural products; they are not fed growth hormones, additives of any kind, or antibiotics. Their bacon and hams are smoked over whisky-flavoured oak chips, having been pickled in brine in the traditional way – unlike some commercial pork, which is pressure pickled.

My favourite cut of pork for roasting is the loin, which produces sweet meat. Chops come from the loin, and there are a number of sauces which complement roast pork or grilled pork chops. Many years ago a

On a bright clear day the sheep are working their way through a field of turnips.

Canadian friend advised me to put tomato purée and dry Vermouth in pork gravy to accompany roast pork, and I have done so ever since. Another excellent sauce combines Madeira with mushrooms, which is a good way of dressing up the simple grilled chop. Pork fillets are, to my mind, so much nicer than veal, providing they come from 'real' pork. They can be sliced in the round, and gently fried in butter with a pinch of rosemary, or they can be slit lengthwise and bashed between pieces of greaseproof paper till they are thin escalopes. These can then be sautéed in butter, or a mixture of butter and oil, and simply served with a squeeze of lemon and ground black pepper, or with a sauce – a good and simple one consists of snipped chives and double cream, boiled with a squeeze of lemon juice.

In casseroles and stews, pork benefits from being combined with spices and fruit to an even greater extent than lamb does. The spiced pork and apricot casserole, for which the recipe is on page 89, is delicious, using one of my favourite spices – cumin. I like to serve this with boiled brown or basmati rice.

Spare ribs of pork make perfect food for the barbecue, especially if served with a sweet and sour barbecue sauce. This can be used to brush the ribs as they cook, and then served as an accompaniment to the cooked ribs.

Offal is an awful word for some of the most delicious bits of these animals. Godfrey loves eating brains, served with black butter, but I'm afraid they don't rate high on my list of personal preferences. Nor do sweetbreads – another of Godfrey's favourites. In fact, on a visit to France he ate sweetbreads for dinner on three consecutive nights. But kidneys and liver – these are the offal I love. In fact they fall into the category of food you either love or loathe. Certainly, when lambs' kidneys are on our menu here at Kinloch (we usually serve them with a port and grainy mustard sauce), they are greeted with glee by a number of our guests. Lamb's liver is good, sautéed briefly in oil and butter and served with sautéed onions and grilled bacon, but calves' liver is the best of all offal. All liver and lambs' kidneys need very little cooking. Cooked for too long, they become tough, and their flavour is impaired. Ox kidney, on the other hand, the kidney used for making steak and kidney pies and puddings, needs long and gentle cooking to tenderize it.

I know of people who haven't eaten red meat for years, yet who sample our meat and enjoy every mouthful. I hasten to add that we love providing meat-free meals for confirmed non-meat-eaters, but luckily there are 'floating voters' who try Scottish meat, out of a curiosity, and then come back for more!

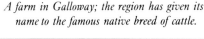

A farm in Galloway; the region has given its name to the famous native breed of cattle.

OXTAIL STEW

The secret of a good oxtail stew is the length of time taken to cook it. The meat should be literally falling off the bones of each piece of oxtail. I usually serve it with creamy mashed potatoes and cabbage or Brussels sprouts.

Serves 8

2 oxtails, cut into pieces
6 tbsp sunflower or other mild oil
3 onions, peeled and chopped
3 carrots, peeled and chopped
2 parsnips, peeled and chopped
½ turnip, peeled and chopped
2 tbsp plain (all-purpose) flour
1½ pints / 3¾ cups / 900ml water and red wine
− I leave the ratio up to you but I use 2 measures of wine to 1 measure of water
2 tbsp tomato paste
1 large garlic clove, peeled and finely chopped
salt and freshly ground pepper

Trim the pieces of oxtail of excess fat, and put them in a saucepan. Pour in cold water to cover the oxtail pieces, and bring the water to simmering point. Drain, rinse the rather unpleasant scum off the pieces of oxtail and pat dry with kitchen paper.

In a large flameproof casserole, heat 4 tbsp of oil and brown the pieces of oxtail all over, removing them to a warm dish as they brown. Heat the remaining oil in the casserole, add the chopped onions and cook gently, stirring occasionally, until soft and translucent. Add the chopped carrots, parsnips and turnip and cook for a further 5 minutes, then stir in the flour and cook for a minute or two before stirring in the water and wine, tomato paste, chopped garlic, and salt and pepper to taste. Let the liquid come to simmering point, then replace the browned pieces of oxtail in the casserole, pushing them down into the liquid and vegetables.

Cover the dish with a lid, and cook in a preheated low oven (300°F / 150°C / gas 2) for 3 hours. Take the casserole out of the oven, let it cool completely, and store it in the refrigerator until you want to serve it.

Before serving, cook in a preheated moderate oven (350°F / 180°C / gas 4) for a further hour.

SPICED PORK CASSEROLED WITH APRICOTS

Don't be tempted to use ready-ground coriander and cumin in this recipe. They just don't have the same pungent flavour that whole spices do. The spices and apricots complement each other and the pork so well. I like to serve this casserole with boiled basmati rice.

Serves 8

1 tbsp each coriander seeds, cumin seeds and ground cinnamon
2 tbsp sunflower oil
2oz / 4 tbsp / 60g butter
3lb / 1·4kg boneless pork −
I use pork from the leg −
cut into 1½ inch / 4cm pieces
3 onions, peeled and sliced
1½ tbsp plain (all-purpose) flour
8oz / 225g dried apricots, soaked overnight in 1½−2 pints /
3¾−5 cups / 900ml−1·25 litres water
1 garlic clove, peeled and finely chopped
salt and freshly ground black pepper

Pound the spices together until they are ground down − in a pestle and mortar, if you have one, or in a small bowl with the end of a rolling pin.

Heat the oil and butter in a flame-proof casserole, and brown the chunks of meat all over, removing them to a warm dish as they brown. Add the sliced onions to the casserole and cook until they are soft and translucent. Stir in the flour and let it cook for a minute or two, then stir in the liquid in which the apricots soaked overnight, and add the apricots too, along with the garlic. Stir in the spices, and season to taste with salt and pepper. Let the liquid bubble gently, then return the browned pork to the casserole. Cover the dish with a lid, and cook for 1½ hours in a preheated moderate oven (350°F / 180°C / gas 4).

MEATBALLS WITH TOMATO AND PIMIENTO SAUCE

'Meatballs' sounds so ugly, but 'rissoles' sounds even worse! Perhaps we should call these polpettone, as in Italy. These are good served with mashed potatoes, and with a stir-fried green vegetable, such as finely shredded cabbage, and grainy mustard.

Serves 8

2 tbsp olive oil
2 onions, peeled and extremely finely chopped
2½lb / 1·2kg best minced beef
(lean ground round)
2oz / 1⅓ cups / 60g fresh white breadcrumbs
2 tbsp grated Parmesan cheese
salt and freshly ground black pepper
sunflower or olive oil for frying

Tomato and pimiento sauce

2 tbsp olive oil
1 onion, peeled and chopped
1 sweet red pepper, core and seeds removed, chopped
1 large garlic clove, peeled and chopped
12 fresh ripe tomatoes, halved,
or 2 14oz / 400g cans
(when fresh tomatoes are tasteless)
pinch of sugar
salt and freshly ground black pepper

For the meatballs, heat the oil in a wide saucepan and cook the very finely chopped onions for about 5 minutes. Take the pan off the heat and let the onions cool completely before mixing them with all the other meatball ingredients. Form into small balls, about the size of a walnut, and put the balls on to a baking sheet lined with greaseproof (wax) paper. These can be frozen at this stage.

To make the sauce, heat the oil and add the chopped onion and red pepper. Cook for about 10 minutes, stirring occasionally, then add the chopped garlic, tomatoes and sugar. Season to taste with salt and pepper. Simmer the sauce gently for 25–30 minutes. Liquidize and sieve the sauce, and reheat when ready to serve with the meatballs.

To cook the meatballs, heat oil in a frying pan to a depth of $\frac{1}{4}$ inch / 5mm. Fry the meatballs until they are well browned all over. As they are cooked keep them warm on kitchen paper on a serving dish in a low oven.

Stir-fried Rump Steak with Red and Yellow Peppers and Fresh Ginger

This recipe takes only minutes to cook, and rather longer to prepare, but the preparation can be done several hours in advance. It really is a dish which can be categorized as convenience food, with none of the unhealthy connotations usually ascribed to the term! The combination of flavours is delicious. I like to serve either basmati or brown rice with this stir-fry.

Serves 8

$2\frac{1}{2}$lb / 1·2kg rump
(US boneless sirloin) steak
3 red and 3 yellow sweet peppers,
core and seeds removed
about 12 spring onions (scallions)
2–3 inch / 5–7·5cm piece fresh root
ginger
sunflower oil
5 tbsp good soy sauce
freshly ground black pepper

Be sure to use a very sharp knife for the preparation as it takes all the effort out of the fine slicing which follows. Slice the steak into thin matchsticks, as for Beef Stroganoff. Slice the peppers into thin strips. Trim the spring onions (scallions)

but leave as much green stalk as possible, and slice them into thin slivers. Peel the ginger and slice it into slivers.

In a wok, if you have one and gas flames to cook on, or in a large frying pan, heat enough sunflower oil to very thinly cover the bottom of the pan, until the oil is smoking hot. Cook the beef, turning it (stir-frying it) until it is sealed all over, removing it to a warm dish as it is browned. Cook the peppers, onions and ginger, for 2 minutes over a really high heat, then return the beef to the pan. Measure in the soy sauce, and cook for a further 1–2 minutes. Season with a good grinding of pepper (no salt as the soy sauce is salty enough), and serve.

Irish Stew with Black Pudding

Technically an Irish Stew doesn't list black pudding as one of its ingredients, nor does Irish Stew, properly made, contain turnip, but I like both in mine. The black pudding makes the stew rich and thickens the juices. You just can't overcook Irish stew – the meat needs to be cooked until it falls off the bones.

Serves 8

$\frac{1}{2}$ medium-sized turnip, peeled and
chopped into small pieces
6 carrots, peeled and sliced
4 onions, peeled and sliced
8 potatoes, peeled and sliced
3lb / 1·4kg neck of lamb, trimmed of its
fattier bits
$1\frac{1}{2}$lb / 700g black pudding,
cut into small cubes
salt and freshly ground black pepper

In a large casserole, make a layer of turnips, carrots and onions – about half the total amount. Then add a layer of sliced potatoes, and on top of the potatoes pack the bits of lamb. Over the lamb scatter the cubed black pudding. Cover that with the remaining onions and carrots, and finish up with the rest of the sliced potatoes.

Season well with salt and pepper, and pour in water to come just below the level of the top of the potatoes. Cover the casserole with a lid and put it into a preheated moderate oven (350°F / 180°C / gas 4) to cook for 3 hours. Take it out of the oven and cool completely – overnight is ideal – then skim any fat off the surface. Reheat in a moderate oven for 1–2 hours, with the lid off the casserole for the last 45 minutes of cooking.

Roast Leg of Lamb with Rosemary and Red Wine Gravy and Blackcurrant and Applemint Jelly

The vogue is for roasted meat (and game, for that matter) to be cooked rare, seemingly no matter what the meat. I do love pink roast beef, but lamb I like cooked to the point where it is barely pink, almost cooked through. It is a matter of personal taste but I recommend 20 minutes to each 1lb / 450g weight.

Serves 8–10

1 leg of lamb
2–3 garlic cloves,
peeled and cut into slivers
freshly ground black pepper
several sprigs of rosemary
2oz / 7 tbsp / 60g plain (all-purpose) flour
$1\frac{1}{2}$–2 pints / $3\frac{3}{4}$–5 cups / 900ml–1·25
litres mixed vegetable stock and
red wine – I leave the ratio up to you
but I use about half and half
2 tsp redcurrant jelly

Jelly

2lb / 3 pints / 900g blackcurrants
2 pints / 5 cups / 1·25 litres water
good handful of fresh mint, preferably
applemint
about 2lb / $4\frac{1}{2}$ cups / 900g granulated or
preserving sugar

First make the jelly. Put the blackcurrants (still on their stalks), water and mint (stalks and all) into a large saucepan and, over moderate heat, bring the water slowly to simmering point. Simmer for about 30 minutes, then strain through a jelly bag, mashing the currants down well. Let the juice drip for several hours, until the contents of the jelly bag are dry. Measure the liquid into a saucepan, and add 1lb / 2 cups / 450g of sugar for each 1 pint / $2\frac{1}{2}$ cups / 600ml of liquid. Over gentle to moderate heat, dissolve the sugar, taking care not to let the liquid boil before the sugar is completely dissolved, then boil fast for 15 minutes. Remove from the heat, drip some of the liquid jelly on to a saucer and leave to cool for several minutes, then push the jelly with the tip of your finger; if the surface wrinkles, you have a set jelly. If it doesn't wrinkle, continue boiling. Pot into warmed jars and seal.

Trim any excess fat off the lamb. With the point of a sharp knife, make small cuts in several places, and stick slivers of garlic into the cuts. Put the lamb in a roasting tin, grind black pepper over it, and lay the sprigs of rosemary over the meat. Roast in a preheated hot oven (425°F / 220°C / gas 7) for 20 minutes to each 1lb / 450g. (Also allow enough time before serving for the lamb to be taken out of the oven and left to sit for 15 minutes – this will make the meat much easier to carve, as the juices settle.)

After the meat is cooked, lift it out of the roasting tin and on to a warmed ashet or serving plate. Cover loosely with foil and leave to rest for 15 minutes. Put the roasting tin containing the lamb fat and juices over a moderate heat and sprinkle in the flour. With a wire whisk, scrape the flour and fat together and cook for a couple of minutes, then pour in the stock and wine mixture and the redcurrant jelly. Stir with the wire whisk until the gravy boils. Don't worry if there are some small lumps in it. Once the gravy has boiled, strain it into a saucepan to reheat. Serve accompanying the carved lamb, with the blackcurrant and applemint jelly.

Cold fillet of roast beef with crème fraîche, decorated with red and yellow peppers.

COLD ROAST FILLET OF BEEF WITH CREME FRAICHE, HORSERADISH AND MUSHROOM SAUCE

As I've already said in the chapter on meat, here in Scotland we have the best beef in the world, providing that we seek out and buy native, homebred beef. One of my favourites is Highland beef. In this recipe, the fillet is roasted (or you can barbecue it), cooled and sliced, and has a simple but delicious sauce spooned over it. The bulk of the sauce consists of crème fraîche which contains much less fat than double (heavy) cream and it tastes wonderfully creamy. If you use 2 fillets of beef you will have some left over, but that is no hardship come the following day.

Serves 8

1 or 2 fillets of beef (beef tenderloin), depending on their size
freshly ground black pepper
2 tbsp sunflower oil
12oz / 350g mushrooms, sliced
1 tbsp freshly grated horseradish
12oz / $1\frac{1}{2}$ cups / 350g crème fraîche
1 tbsp finely chopped parsley

Trim the beef and grind plenty of black pepper over it. Roast it in a preheated hot oven (425°F / 220°C / gas 7), allowing 10 minutes to each 1lb / 450g plus an extra 10 minutes, for rare beef. If you like the meat slightly better cooked, just give it a bit more cooking time per 1lb / 450g. Allow the beef to cool.

To make the sauce, heat the oil in a frying pan until it is very hot, add the mushrooms and cook over a high heat until the mushrooms are positively crisp – the flavour is much nicer. Cool the mushrooms.

Stir the horseradish into the crème fraîche, and fold in the cold mushrooms.

When the beef is cold, slice it thinly and arrange down a serving plate. Spoon the sauce over. Sprinkle the chopped parsley (you can add snipped chives, too, if you like) down the centre.

GLORIOUS GAME

Because of the dates of the various game seasons,
game is essentially an autumn and winter food item,
and among the loudest heralds of autumn are the
arrivals of the first grouse and several weeks later,
pheasant. Guests at this time of year anticipate
sampling the best game that Scotland has to offer, and
I love to cook it, in all its various guises. We get
venison, hare, grouse, pheasant, black game, partridge
and wild duck; and when the weather is
cold enough, woodcock and snipe abound around the
shores here at Kinloch.

Opposite: Eric Allen in one of the drawing-rooms at
Airds Hotel. Above: A classic hunting scene from Airds.

OTHER game birds are indigenous to Scotland, such as capercailie, or wood-grouse, which is a sort of wild turkey with a flavour reminiscent of turpentine, so I'm told, owing to the fact that they live in pine forests and feed off the pine needles. They are fairly rare, however, and don't ever feature on our menu here at Kinloch. Nor do ptarmigan, small grey birds which turn white in winter. Ptarmigan are of the grouse family, and live above the snow line. There are ptarmigan on the top of the hill behind Kinloch, but the time it takes to climb up so far, without any certainty of returning home with enough birds to put on the menu, makes ptarmigan a non-starter when it comes to menu planning!

All the game apart from red and roe venison, woodcock and snipe comes to us from Duncan Fraser, our excellent game dealer in Inverness. He also supplies us with hares. Duncan has been a game dealer for thirty years. The firm is an old family one of butcher and fishmonger, and his two sons now work in the business with him.

We get pigeon all year round, which fact I think means that they cannot technically be called game, but Duncan Fraser supplies us with excellent plump little pigeon. And one other item which I never cook (but which Godfrey loves to eat – poor him!) and which I have great difficulty in thinking of as game, is rabbit. The reason why I can't bring myself to cook rabbit is that I can't bear to eat them, and I can't bear to eat them because I can't get the memory of poor little rabbits dying most revoltingly from myximatosis out of my mind. I can never cook anything which I can't eat. (In fact the only other thing I don't ever make because I don't enjoy eating it is cheesecake.)

The demand for game is increasing. I'm sure this is due partly to the fact that game is unadulterated, lean and therefore low in cholesterol. There is also no doubt that people who might not previously have bothered to cook

Above: One of the fine game paintings from Pittodrie House Hotel. Opposite: A beautiful still-life of game birds including grouse, pheasant, quail and mallard.

game are now being tempted by its availability in good supermarkets. This is because nowadays venison, pheasant and duck (mallard) are quite extensively farmed. Farmed birds and meat haven't got the same flavour as wild, but they are very good, not expensive and, most important, they are available. Much of our game in Scotland is now exported to Germany. The German people love to eat game, and since Chernobyl there is no demand for game from within Germany, so they import it from here. Duncan Fraser, of Inverness, now has an agent in Hamburg, and although his main buyers are in Hamburg and Munich, he also sells to smaller outlets throughout Germany. The game he exports are venison (red and roe deer), pheasant and partridge. When he decided to start exporting game, German veterinary surgeons had to come over to inspect the quality of the game he deals in as well as his premises, before he could be issued with an official export licence.

Venison is a big subject. Mostly, we use venison from red deer (all the venison we use is wild) and this is shot on the hill behind our house. Like all meat, venison needs to be hung. We hang our venison haunches for up to 21 days, depending on the weather. If the temperature is mild, 21 days is too long, and 12–14 would be about right. And hanging means just that – the meat should be suspended, high up to be safe from the unwanted attentions of any animals tempted by the scent of the meat. If flies are a problem, one can cover the meat in muslin before hanging. The main thing to remember is that there should be good air circulation around the hanging meat. Proper hanging makes venison one of the best of meats, but insufficiently hung venison can put people off for life! If you are buying venison, whether from a game dealer, a butcher, or a supermarket, ask the person selling it whether it has been hung, and if so, for how long.

We buy Sika venison from Duncan Fraser. Sika are

Prized firearms, such as the beautiful example above,
are often handed down from generation to generation.

smaller than red deer, and the meat is slightly fattier. I think of Sika venison as being somewhere between red and roe. We very occasionally get roe, and this meat is so tender you can cut it with the side of a fork. It is delicious – if, that is, you can banish from your mind the vision of the enchanting animals from which it comes! I'm ashamed to say that I can. They are wicked marauders, which is why they get shot in the first place, because of the harm they do to trees, plantations and gardens.

The season for stalking red deer stags (males) starts on 1 July and ends in mid October. For hinds (females) in Scotland, the culling (shooting) season is from 21 October to 15 February. Farmed venison is available all year round. This meat is more tender, but it lacks the flavour of wild venison.

The cuts of venison are as varied as those from any other animal, but the most usually found is the haunch, which, if from a red deer, will be too large unless you are planning to serve it to around 20 people! Haunches are also sold in halves, however. The fillet, steaks cut from the leg or loin, and the saddle are other common cuts.

Venison is a meat with very little fat and virtually no marbling of fat through it. There is a tendency, as a result, for the meat to be dry when cooked. There are several ways to overcome this; one is to lard the meat with pieces of fat. Properly done, this means using lardons of fat, usually cut from the back fat of a loin of pork, and threaded into the venison using a larding needle. Not many people have a larding needle these days, but just the same results can be had from making little slits in the meat with the point of a very sharp knife, and pushing slivers of fat into the slits. Alternatively, you can lay strips of fat over the meat.

The method we use to roast venison here at Kinloch is described in the recipe given on page 107, for roast haunch of Sika. We roast the meat on a bed of vegetables which have been sautéed in oil (or beef dripping) and covering the meat with more vegetables. The meat is roast in a hot oven for the first half-hour, then red wine is poured around the meat, the roasting tin and its contents are covered tightly with foil, and the meat is then cooked at a lower temperature for the remainder of its cooking time. This produces moist venison.

Some people think that venison needs to be marinaded before being cooked; I am not of this opinion, but there are definitely occasions when certain cuts of meat benefit from a good marinade – anything from 6 hours to 48 hours in a well-flavoured marinade. For example, I would certainly marinade venison steaks which were intended to be grilled or sautéed in butter and oil, or even barbecued.

Venison, particularly from red deer, is strong-flavoured meat. It makes the most delicious stews and casseroles, and whether roast, sautéed in the form of steaks, or casseroled, it benefits from having sweet and sharp flavours combined with it. Root vegetables, particularly puréed, go well with venison, and spiced red cabbage, cooked with apples and onions, is one of the best accompaniments I know. Rowan jelly or redcurrant jelly is delicious, too, served with roast venison of all cuts.

Leftovers from a roast can be minced, or whizzed in

a food processor, and made into delicious shepherds pie; for this, rather than the traditional mashed potatoes, I like to put steamed leeks in a white sauce over the minced venison. Alternatively, you can make a very good crumbled top using oatmeal.

Venison burgers are widely available, from butchers, game dealers and supermarkets. These are good, but tend to be on the dry side. In the same way, venison sausages are as good as the recipe used to make them. Duncan Fraser makes very good venison sausages, and so does Michael Gibson, whose recipe includes berries such as blackberries when they are in season. Michael Gibson (see the chapter on meat) also makes delicious sausages from smoked venison. There is more about smoked venison in the chapter on smoking!

There is something almost magical about hares. I love seeing them, but they are also wonderful to eat. There are two types of hare, brown hare and blue, or mountain hare. We only get brown hare from Duncan Fraser, and whenever I have eaten blue hare I have been disappointed. Hare are at their best between October and March. The flavour of hare is strong and gamy, and I love it. Hares should be hung, head down and ungutted for about ten days – or a bit more or a bit less, depending on the weather. A bowl should be placed beneath the hare, to catch any blood dripping from it. You can prevent the blood from coagulating by adding a few drops of wine vinegar to the bowl. This blood is used to enrich the sauce with which the hare is served. By the way, the blood freezes satisfactorily, if you plan to freeze the hare once hung, rather than cook it straight away.

Probably the best-known recipe for casseroled hare is Jugged Hare, so called from the days when the hare was cooked in a jug, with vegetables packed around it, and the jug in a pan of simmering water. Nowadays Jugged Hare is cooked in a casserole fashion, with the blood stirred into the hot sauce just before serving. Jugged Hare is one of the best winter dishes I know, especially when it is accompanied by forcemeat balls, small walnut-sized balls of breadcrumbs mixed with finely chopped sautéed onions, egg yolk, and lots of grated lemon and chopped parsley.

Roast saddle of hare is delicious, but it needs to be frequently basted throughout its roasting time, to prevent the meat from drying. A saddle of hare will feed about three people. Soured cream and a teaspoon of French

Kinveachy of Seafield Estates is typical of the many trophy-filled hunting lodges.

mustard stirred into the pan juices after the saddle is cooked make a delicious accompanying sauce, and redcurrant or rowan jelly, served with the saddle, adds a needed touch of sweetness.

Hare can combine well with other types of game in stews, game pies and puddings, and hare soup is very good, too.

Perhaps the best known of Scotland's game birds, grouse, or *lagopus scoticus* to give it its Latin name, is a totally wild bird. To my knowledge no one has tried to farm grouse, and I'm not sure that it is even possible. They feed entirely off heather and berries, and are one of Scotland's outstanding gastronomic treats. A good-sized grouse is sufficient for two people, but when they are small you need one per person. Grouse need to be hung, depending on the weather, for anything from three to seven days.

Best of all I like grouse roast; for this they need to be sat on a slice of bread (which is served under the cooked grouse), and their breasts must be covered with strips of streaky bacon to prevent the meat from drying out during cooking. In a hot oven, grouse take 20–25 minutes to roast. This will leave the meat barely pink. I don't like the current vogue for undercooking game as well as meat. In this country roast grouse is traditionally served with bread sauce, fried breadcrumbs, and game chips or straw potatoes. Substituting a packet of potato crisps just will not do! I also like to serve rowan and apple jelly with the grouse. A simple green vegetable, such as steamed broccoli, is the perfect vegetable accompaniment. Game gravy needs to be thin, and I like to add port to mine.

Grouse for roasting have to be young birds. Godfrey tells me that you can tell a young grouse from an old one by its beak: the beak of a young bird is soft. You can also tell the difference by their wing features, which in a young bird are not yet formed. However, the best way is to trust your game dealer! There are numerous dishes to be made from old grouse, which need much longer and slower cooking than young. They can be combined with other game in game stews, or game pies or puddings.

Pheasant are in season from 1 October until 1 February. Native to Scotland, they are now extensively farmed, but farmed pheasant are a different bird, flavourwise, to wild, which are greatly superior in taste. Farmed pheasant and hand-reared pheasant are both heavily corn-fed – you can tell a corn-fed bird by the thick band of yellow fat between the skin and the breast. Both wild and farmed birds need the same amount of hanging, but, as always, the length of time depends on the weather. If the weather is cold, they need as much as 12–14 days' hanging time, but if it is mild, 4–7 days would be enough.

Pheasants look spectacularly beautiful – at least, the cock pheasants do! They have brilliant copper and gold plumage, with long tail feathers, whereas the brown hen pheasant is rather a drab little creature. In the autumn months pheasants are to be seen all over Scotland – often, sadly, as corpses on main roads, which they fail to cross quickly enough. Roast pheasant can be delicious, but golly, it can also be dull. The birds need to be hung (ask when you buy them) and to have strips of streaky bacon across their breasts. I like to stuff them with mush-rooms or chanterelles sautéed in butter. I roast pheasants in a hot oven for ten minutes, then I lower the temperature to moderate (350°F/180°C/gas 4) for the remainder of the cooking time, about 25–30 minutes. A hen pheasant will serve two people, a cock three, at a pinch, and if it is on the large side, four. Roast pheasant, like grouse, is served with bread sauce and game chips or straw potatoes, and I like a combination of root vegetables, such as carrots, parsnips and celeriac, or jerusalem artichokes, cut in strips and slowly cooked in a mixture of butter and oil.

There are numerous other ways to cook pheasant. One of my favourites is with apples, fresh ginger and Calvados (or you can use cider), but the flavour of pheasant goes so well with virtually everything I can think of – chestnuts and orange, in a casserole, or roast with a soured cream and sautéed mushroom sauce, which makes a break from the more traditional roast pheasant. Pheasant carcases, like any game carcase, should never be wasted. They can go into a stockpot to make stock for game soup, one of the best of all winter soups.

The season for black game is from 20 August until 10 December. We don't get them often, and we have always been lucky and had young birds. They need hanging for two or three days longer than a grouse – they belong to the grouse family, and they tend to dryness. For roasting, I cover their breasts with streaky bacon, stick about two ounces of butter inside each bird, and roast them at a high temperature for ten minutes, then I pour about a pint of red wine around them, cover the roasting tin and its contents with foil and continue to cook the birds at a moderate temperature for a further 35–40 minutes. A black cock will feed three people, a hen (they are called greyhens) two.

Partridge are in season from 1 September to 1 February. Partridge are my favourite of all game birds to eat, providing they are grey-legged partridge and not the other sort, the red-legged ones, which are altogether dreary and disappointing to eat. I feel an awful hypocrite saying that partridge are my favourite eating birds, because they are such enchanting birds alive. This doesn't, however, prevent my enjoyment of them on the plate! They are best served roast, and one bird feeds one person. A partridge needs comparatively little hanging time – depending on the weather, from three to six days. Partridge are relatively rare these days, and their flavour is exquisite. Because of their distinct flavour, I don't like to cover their breasts with bacon to roast them, I prefer to rub butter into each instead, and to baste them at frequent intervals. Roasting in a fairly hot oven (400°F/200°C/gas 6), for 30 minutes is enough cooking time, and you can serve them with bread sauce, game chips, etc. in the traditional way, or with roast parsnips, whose sweetness of flavour seems to complement the partridge perfectly, red cabbage with apples and onions, and creamy mashed potatoes.

Snipe are in season from 12 August, and woodcock from 1 October, and for both the season ends on 31 January. Snipe live in bogs, and woodcock like scrubby dampish terrain. We have both around us here at Kinloch, but woodcock only when there is a real drop in

temperature; the cold weather brings them down from high ground to our (sea) level, where they can be sure to get their beaks into the ground to feed. They both feed off the same things, and both have long beaks. They are small birds, and one per person is a serving for cooked woodcock or snipe.

Roast woodcock, which Godfrey likes best of all game, need very short hanging – just two or three days – and they must be roast intact, that is to say, ungutted. Rub butter into each bird, cover the breasts with a strip of streaky bacon, and roast them in a hot oven (425°F/220°C/gas 7), for 12–15 minutes. Serve them with croutons, bread fried in butter till golden on each side. The woodcock devotees (I am not one) then scoop out the brains and the entrails and mash them together

Below: Despite his magnificent antlers, this is a young red deer stag.
Overleaf: spring snow glistens on Glen Coe.

This grouse and pigeon terrine makes an ideal first course
and is delicious with Cumberland jelly or soft fruit.

on the crouton, to eat with the flesh of the little bird. When scooping out the entrails, take care to remove what Godfrey refers to as the 'gritty bag', which is in fact the stomach.

Snipe are also roasted intact, but with their beak pushed into the body. As with woodcock, snipe are served with a crouton, and the brains and entrails are eaten.

Teal is my favourite wild duck to eat, but we don't get very many of them. Apart from being delicious, a plump teal is just the right size for one person. The wild duck we regularly cook are mallard. As with all duck, mallard have a broad flat breastbone, and a mallard will comfortably serve two people, three at a pinch. The

season for mallard is from 1 September until 20 February. Because duck tend to have a fishy taste if shot on the shore, it is a good idea to put half an onion and a piece of peeled (raw) potato inside each bird before roasting. The flavour improves with hanging, and they should hang for up to a week, depending, as ever, on the weather.

Mallard are roast in a hot oven (425°F/220°C/gas 7), for about 30 minutes. They benefit from a rich orangey sauce. I add flour to the juices in the pan after the birds are cooked, and I stir in red wine and water or stock, a tablespoon of marmalade or honey, and the segments of two or three oranges. Butter is rubbed fairly thickly over each bird before roasting.

MARINADE FOR VENISON OR HARE

This recipe makes sufficient marinade for a haunch of red deer or two (smaller) haunches of Sika deer or two jointed hares.

6 tbsp olive or sunflower oil
2 onions, peeled and quartered
1 celery stick, quartered
handful of bashed parsley stalks (stems)
pared rind of 1 orange
4–6 juniper berries, bashed with the end of a rolling pin
good pinch of dried thyme, or
1 sprig of fresh thyme
$\frac{1}{2}$ tsp rock salt (kosher salt)
freshly ground black pepper
1 pint / $2\frac{1}{2}$ cups / 600ml red wine

Heat the oil in a saucepan and add the vegetables, parsley, pared orange rind, juniper berries, thyme, salt and a good grinding of pepper. Cook for about 5 minutes, then pour in the wine. Simmer gently for 2–3 minutes, then take the marinade off the heat and cool completely before pouring over the meat in a dish. Turn the meat over in the marinade every few hours, and keep it in a cool place, ideally a larder.

PHEASANT CASSEROLED WITH CHESTNUTS AND MADEIRA

This is the most delicious way of cooking pheasant, especially welcome when there is a glut of birds and you are wondering how on earth to tempt some pheasant-jaded palates!

Serves 8

2oz / 4 tbsp / 60g butter
4 tbsp sunflower or other mild oil
2 oven-ready pheasants
3 onions, peeled and finely sliced
2oz / scant $\frac{1}{2}$ cup / 60g plain (all-purpose) flour

2 pints / 5 cups / 1·25 litres mixed water and Madeira – I leave the ratio up to you, but I use about $\frac{1}{2}$ pint / $1\frac{1}{4}$ cups / 300ml Madeira
1 15oz / 425g can chestnuts (unsweetened), drained of their liquid
grated rind of 1 orange
salt and freshly ground black pepper

Heat the butter and oil in a heavy flame-proof casserole. Brown the pheasants all over, then remove them and keep them warm while you carry on with the recipe. Add the sliced onions to the fat in the casserole, and cook them until they are soft and translucent, 5–10 minutes. Stir in the flour and let it cook for a couple of minutes before adding the liquid. Stir continuously until the sauce boils.

Replace the pheasants in the liquid, cover the casserole with a lid and cook in a preheated moderate oven (350°F / 180°C / gas 4) for an hour. Test to see if the pheasants are cooked by sticking the point of a sharp knife into the thigh; if the juices run tinged with pink, continue to cook the pheasants for a further 10 minutes.

When they are cooked, take the pheasants out of the sauce, draining them well, and carve all the meat from the birds. Put the pheasant meat back into the casserole, and stir in the chestnuts and grated orange rind. Season to taste with salt and pepper, and gently reheat before serving.

CASSEROLE OF VENISON WITH PRUNES AND PICKLED WALNUTS

The prunes and pickled walnuts provide just the sweet and sharp contrast that complements the flavour of venison so well.

Serves 8

2 rounded tbsp plain (all-purpose) flour
$\frac{1}{2}$ tsp salt

freshly ground black pepper
3lb / 1·4kg boneless venison, cut into $1\frac{1}{2}$ inch / 4cm chunks
about 4 tbsp sunflower or other mild oil
3 onions, peeled and finely sliced
1 pint / $2\frac{1}{2}$ cups / 600ml each red wine and water
1 15oz / 425g jar pickled walnuts, drained of their brine
8 prunes, soaked until soft, then stoned and chopped

Put the flour, salt and a good grinding of pepper into a bowl. Toss the pieces of venison in the seasoned flour to coat. Heat the oil in a heavy flameproof casserole and brown the meat, a few pieces at a time; remove the browned meat and keep it warm while you brown the rest. When all the meat is browned, add the onions to the casserole and cook them until they are soft and translucent, 5–10 minutes. Stir in the wine and water, scraping the bits off the bottom of the casserole with a wooden spoon. When the liquid is simmering, replace the browned meat in the casserole, and stir in the pickled walnuts and prunes.

Cover the casserole with a lid, and cook in a preheated moderate oven (350°F / 180°C / gas 4) for an hour. Let the casserole cool completely, then store in the refrigerator overnight. Cook it for a further hour at the same temperature before serving. All stews and casseroles benefit in flavour from reheating.

SPICED RED CABBAGE WITH ONIONS AND APPLES

This is such a perfect vegetable dish to serve with game, but especially with venison, hare and partridge.

Serves 8

1 red cabbage, or 2 if they are particularly small ones
4 tbsp sunflower, olive or other mild oil

2 onions, peeled and chopped
3 good eating apples,
cored and chopped
salt and freshly ground black pepper
$\frac{1}{2}$ tsp ground allspice
1 tbsp wine vinegar

Discard the outer leaves of the cabbage and shred finely. Heat the oil in a flame-proof casserole and cook the chopped onions for about 5 minutes, stirring them from time to time. Add the shredded cabbage and chopped apples and cook, stirring occasionally, for 10 minutes. Season to taste with salt and pepper.

Add the allspice and wine vinegar – white or red, it doesn't matter – and put a lid on the casserole. Cook over a gentle heat for 20 minutes, stirring occasionally.

This cabbage dish can be kept warm for half an hour or even longer before serving.

BREAD SAUCE

The seasoning of bread sauce is a matter of taste, but this is how we make bread sauce at Kinloch. It freezes beautifully.

Serves 8

$\frac{1}{2}$ loaf day-old white bread,
baked not steamed
$1\frac{1}{2}$ pints / $3\frac{3}{4}$ cups / 900ml milk
2 onions, peeled and each stuck
with 6 cloves
$\frac{1}{2}$ tsp salt
freshly ground black pepper
2oz / 4tbsp / 60g butter

Cut the crusts off the loaf, and make the bread into crumbs. This is easiest done in a food processor.

Put the milk and clove-studded onions in a saucepan over a gentle heat, and heat until a skin forms on the milk. Take the milk off the heat and leave it for an hour or two to infuse with the flavours of the onions and cloves.

Add the breadcrumbs to the milk and heat gently for 20 minutes. Season with salt and a good grinding of pepper, and stir in the butter, cut into bits. The sauce shouldn't be too stiff in texture – if it is, add a little more milk. Discard onion and cloves before serving with roast game.

PHEASANT BREASTS WITH APPLES, GINGER AND CALVADOS

This is an ideal way to serve pheasant. I know that to cut off the breasts of the pheasant may sound extravagant, but you can use the rest of the meat for the pheasant and pigeon terrine and the carcase for making game soup. This recipe is quite quick to prepare, and I like to serve it with creamy mashed potatoes and spiced red cabbage with onions and apples.

Serves 8

2oz / 4 tbsp / 60g butter
2 tbsp sunflower oil
breasts from 4 pheasants
2 onions, peeled and very thinly sliced
4 good eating apples –
NOT Golden Delicious, which taste of nothing – peeled, cored
and thinly sliced (squeeze lemon juice over the slices to prevent them from discolouring)
2 inch / 5cm piece of fresh root ginger, peeled and cut into fine slivers
1 tbsp plain (all-purpose) flour
1 pint / $2\frac{1}{2}$ cups / 600ml chicken stock
salt and freshly ground white or black pepper
3 tbsp Calvados

Heat the butter and oil in a large flame-proof casserole. Brown the pheasant breasts on each side, then remove them to a warm dish. Add the sliced onions to the casserole and cook until they are soft and translucent. Add the sliced apples and slivers of fresh ginger and cook for a minute or two, then stir in the flour and cook for a further minute or two. Gradually add the stock, stirring continuously until the sauce boils. Season to taste with salt and pepper.

Replace the pheasant breasts in the casserole, cover with a lid and cook in a preheated moderate, oven (350°F / 180°C / gas 4) for 35–40 minutes.

Stir the Calvados into the sauce just before serving. This dish can be kept warm for up to an hour, at a low temperature in the oven.

PHEASANT AND PIGEON TERRINE WITH CUMBERLAND JELLY

This makes a delicious first course, and a convenient one, too, as it has to be prepared a day or two in advance. The Cumberland jelly can be made a couple of weeks ahead and kept in the refrigerator.

Serves 8

3 tbsp olive oil
2 onions, peeled and very finely chopped
1 garlic clove, peeled and
very finely chopped
grated rind of 1 lemon
freshly ground black pepper
2 sprigs of fresh thyme,
or $\frac{1}{2}$ tsp dried thyme
7fl oz / 1 cup / 200ml port wine
$1\frac{1}{2}$lb / 700g pigeon and pheasant meat, finely diced
1lb / 450g Lincoln sausages
(fresh pork link sausages,
or other herby or seasoned sausages)
12–14 streaky bacon rashers
(US bacon slices)

Cumberland jelly

2 tsp mustard powder
$\frac{1}{4}$ pint / $\frac{2}{3}$ cup / 150ml port wine
grated rind and juice of 1 lemon and 1 orange
2 tsp unflavoured gelatine powder
8oz / $\frac{3}{4}$ cup / 225g redcurrant jelly

To make the Cumberland jelly, put all the ingredients in a saucepan. Over moderate heat melt the jelly – this takes a surprising length of time, but don't be tempted to raise the heat and hurry up the task or the jelly will just burn! Once everything is melted together, pour into a warmed jar, cover and seal.

Heat the oil, add the onions and garlic and cook for a couple of minutes, then add the grated lemon rind, plenty of pepper, the leaves from the thyme sprigs, or dried thyme, and the port. Let the mixture boil fast for 3–4 minutes then take the pan off the heat and leave to cool completely.

In a bowl, mix together the diced game, the pork sausage meat and the cold port wine mixture, using your hands to mix thoroughly – messy, I know, but the only way to mix properly. Cover the bowl and leave in a cool place for several hours, or overnight – the longer the better.

Meanwhile, prepare a 2lb/900g terrine or loaf tin by lining it with foil. Stretch the bacon with the blade of a knife on a board, and lay the rashers/slices in the inside of the terrine widthways, to line it evenly.

Pack the game mixture into the terrine and cover with foil. Put the terrine into a roasting tin and add enough water to the tin to come halfway up the sides of the terrine. Cook in a preheated moderate oven (350°F / 180°C / gas 4) for $1\frac{3}{4}$–2 hours.

Take the terrine out of the water when the cooking time is up. Weight it – I use cans of tomatoes or similar – and leave it until cold before storing in the refrigerator. Turn out to serve, cut into slices about $\frac{1}{2}$ inch / 1cm thick. Accompany with the Cumberland jelly.

JUGGED HARE WITH FORCEMEAT BALLS

This is one of the best, gamy, rich dishes there is. Served traditionally with forcemeat balls (which, incidentally, freeze

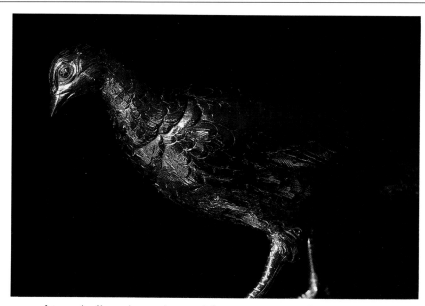

A superb silver pheasant, one of the many treasures from Inverlochy Castle, a hotel with a unique blend of informality and grandeur.

very well), redcurrant jelly, creamed mashed potatoes and a green vegetable like Brussels sprouts, this is a most satisfying dish for chilly winter days.

Serves 8

2 oven-ready hares
2oz / 4 tbsp / 60g butter
3 tbsp sunflower oil
3 onions, peeled and each stuck with a few cloves
3 carrots, peeled and cut in half
2–3 celery sticks, halved
1 garlic clove, peeled and chopped
pared rind of 1 lemon and 1 orange
4–5 juniper berries, bashed with the end of a rolling pin
small handful of black peppercorns
1 tsp rock salt (kosher salt)

For thickening the sauce

2–3oz / 4–6 tbsp / 60–90g butter
2–3oz / 6–9 tbsp / 60–90g plain (all-purpose) flour
1 tbsp redcurrant jelly
$\frac{1}{4}$–$\frac{1}{2}$ pint / $\frac{2}{3}$–$1\frac{1}{4}$ cups / 150–300ml port wine
salt and freshly ground black pepper

Forcemeat balls

1oz / 2 tbsp / 30g butter
1 tbsp sunflower oil
1 onion, peeled and very finely chopped
6oz / 2 cups / 175g day-old breadcrumbs
3oz / 90g shredded beef suet
grated rind of 2 lemons
2 tbsp chopped parsley
1 size 2 / US extra large egg, beaten
flour for coating
sunflower oil for frying

Cut the hares into serving pieces. If available, keep the blood in a bowl to add to the sauce before serving. In a large flame-proof casserole or heavy saucepan, heat the butter and oil until very hot. Pat dry each piece of hare with kitchen paper, to absorb any excess moisture or blood, and brown each piece of hare on both sides in the hot fat. As the pieces are browned, remove them to a warmed dish; keep them warm in a low oven. When all the pieces of hare are browned, add the vegetables and garlic to the fat in the pan and cook for a few minutes.

Replace the pieces of hare in the pan and add the pared lemon and orange rinds, the juniper berries, peppercorns and salt. Pour in enough water to cover the hare. Cover the pan with a tightly fitting lid and cook gently on top of the stove, or in a preheated low oven (300°F / 150°C / gas 2), for about 3 hours, or until the meat is just beginning to come away from the bones.

Meanwhile, make the forcemeat balls. Heat the butter and oil in a saucepan, add the onion and cook for a few minutes. Pour the onion into a mixing bowl and add the breadcrumbs. Mix well, then mix in the suet, lemon rind, parsley and beaten egg. Flour your hands and form the mixture into small balls about the size of a walnut. Coat each ball in flour, and put on a baking sheet lined with greaseproof (wax) paper. Cover and keep in the refrigerator until you are ready to cook them. (They can also be frozen.)

Remove the casserole from the oven and cool the hare in the stock. When cool, take the pieces of hare out of the stock and strip the meat from the bones. Put it into an ovenproof dish and set aside while you make the sauce. Strain the stock.

Use the larger quantities of butter, flour and port wine if you have no hare's blood to thicken the sauce. Melt the butter in a saucepan, add the flour and cook for 2–3 minutes. Gradually add $1\frac{1}{2}$ pints / $3\frac{3}{4}$ cups / 900ml of the hare stock, stirring all the time until the sauce boils. Stir in the redcurrant jelly and port wine, stirring until the jelly has melted in the hot sauce. Season to taste with salt and pepper. Pour the sauce over the hare meat in the ovenproof dish. Cover the dish and reheat in the low oven until the sauce is bubbling gently and does so for 10–15 minutes.

Meanwhile, fry the forcemeat balls. Heat oil in a frying pan and cook the balls until golden brown all over. Drain them on several thicknesses of kitchen paper. They will keep warm for up to an hour.

If thickening the sauce with blood, pour a little of the hot sauce into the bowl containing the blood. Mix well, and stir this into the rest of the sauce and hare in the dish. If necessary, keep in a warm oven until you are ready to serve, but take care not to let the sauce boil again once the blood has been added. Serve the jugged hare with the forcemeat balls.

ROAST WILD DUCK WITH ORANGE AND SAUTERNES SAUCE

Of all wild duck, teal are probably my favourite. If you have access to a supply of teal, this sauce is perfect with them as well as with the mallard in this recipe. I allow one bird between two people, or one per person if they are on the small side.

Serves 6

3 oven-ready mallards or other wild ducks
butter
3 onions, peeled and halved
strips of pared orange rind

Sauce

2oz / 4 tbsp / 60g butter
1 onion, peeled and thinly sliced
grated rind of 2 oranges
1 pint / $2\frac{1}{2}$ cups / 600ml chicken or vegetable stock or water
2 tsp arrowroot mixed with the juice of $\frac{1}{2}$ lemon
salt and freshly ground pepper
$\frac{1}{2}$ pint / $1\frac{1}{4}$ cups / 300ml Sauternes (or another sweet white wine)
2 oranges, peeled, all pith removed and segmented

To roast the birds, rub the skin with butter and inside each put one onion and a few strips of pared orange rind. Put the birds into a roasting tin with 1 pint / $2\frac{1}{2}$ cups / 600ml of water. Roast them in a preheated hot oven (425°F / 220°C / gas 7 for about 45 minutes.

Meanwhile, make the sauce. Melt the butter, add the onion and cook until the onion is soft and translucent. Add the grated orange rind and stock or water.

Bring the liquid to simmering point and simmer for 5 minutes, with the pan uncovered. Stir a little of the hot liquid into the arrowroot and lemon mixture, then pour this back into the saucepan and stir until the sauce boils. The arrowroot gives a clear sauce. Season to taste with salt and pepper, and pour in the Sauternes. (You can make the sauce to this stage in the morning for dinner that evening and just reheat to serve.) Add the orange segments just before serving. Serve the sauce separately.

GAME SOUP

An essential ingredient of game soup is good game stock, so this is a two-stage recipe – first the stock, then the soup. It is an ideal way to use old grouse. Carcases from cooked birds can be used to make the stock, but it is not quite as good as when made with uncooked bones.

Serves 8

Stock
2–3 game carcases, preferably from uncooked birds such as pigeon, grouse or pheasant
4 pints / $2\frac{1}{2}$ quarts / 2·5 litres water
3 onions, peeled and each stuck with a few cloves
2 celery sticks
small handful of black peppercorns
1 tsp rock salt (kosher salt)
1 bouquet garni

Soup

2oz / 4 tbsp / 60g butter
2 bacon rashers (slices), chopped
2 onions, peeled and chopped
2 carrots, peeled and chopped
2 potatoes, peeled and chopped
1 large garlic clove, peeled and chopped
pared rind of $\frac{1}{2}$ lemon and $\frac{1}{2}$ orange
3–4 juniper berries, bashed with the end of a rolling pin
1 tbsp redcurrant jelly
salt and freshly ground black pepper
$\frac{1}{2}$ pint / $1\frac{1}{4}$ cups / 300ml port wine

Put all the stock ingredients into a large saucepan and cover with a lid. If you are using uncooked carcases, bring the water to simmering point, then drain off and measure 4 pints / 2½ quarts / 2·5 litres of fresh water into the pan and bring to a simmering point once more (remember to add another tsp of salt). Once the water has reached a gentle simmer, cook, covered, for 3 hours. Cool, and strain the stock. Keep in the refrigerator and freeze the surplus stock for making game soup another time.

Melt the butter in a large saucepan and add the bacon and onions; cook over moderate heat until the onions are soft and translucent, then add the carrots, potatoes, garlic, lemon and orange rind, and juniper berries. Cook for a further few minutes, then pour in 2 pints / 5 cups / 1·25 litres of the game stock. Half cover the pan with a lid and simmer gently for 40–45 minutes. Cool a bit, then liquidize, adding the redcurrant jelly to the soup in the liquidizer. Sieve the liquidized soup – game soup should be velvety smooth – and season to taste with salt and pepper. Add the port, and reheat to serve, garnished, if you like, with small croûtons mixed with chopped parsley.

This soup freezes very well.

ROAST HAUNCH OF SIKA DEER WITH VEGETABLES, PORT AND REDCURRANT JELLY SAUCE

Sika deer are small, and a haunch of Sika is just the right size for 8 people. Sika is delicious venison; I would place it somewhere between red deer and roe. But all meat needs to be well hung, and Sika is no exception. Depending on the weather, we hang our venison for between 8 and 18 days. In this recipe the meat is roasted on a bed of vegetables which have been sautéed in beef dripping (if you haven't any beef dripping, use olive oil instead). It is accompanied by a sauce made by liquidizing the vegetables with the meat juices, and adding redcurrant jelly and port wine.

Serves 8

4oz / ½ cup / 120g beef dripping, or
6 tbsp olive oil
2 onions, peeled and chopped
2 leeks, sliced
2 carrots, peeled and sliced
2 parsnips, peeled and sliced
about ¼ turnip, peeled and chopped
8oz / 225g mushrooms, chopped
3–4 juniper berries, bashed with the end
of a rolling pin
freshly ground black pepper
1 haunch of Sika deer - about
4–5lbs / 2kg
1 haunch – about 4–5lbs – of Sika deer
½ pint / 1¼ cups / 300ml port wine
¾ pint / 2 cups / 450ml water
1 tbsp redcurrant jelly
salt

Melt the dripping (or heat the oil) in a large saucepan. Add the vegetables, juniper berries and a good grinding of black pepper and cook all together for 7–10 minutes. Pour half the vegetable mixture into the bottom of a roasting tin, put the haunch of deer on top, and pour the remaining vegetables and dripping over the meat. Roast in a preheated hot oven (425°F / 220°C / gas 7) for 30 minutes, then cover the meat and roasting tin tightly with foil and roast for a further 1½ hours.

When the cooking time is up, take the meat out of the tin and put it on a warmed serving plate in a low oven. Stir the port, water and redcurrant jelly into the vegetables and meat juices in the roasting tin and then liquidize the lot. Sieve the liquidized sauce, to get a velvety smoothness, and reheat it in a saucepan. Adjust the seasoning.

Carve the meat and serve with the sauce.

Struy deer farm, near Beauly.

FRUIT, VEGETABLES

—— AND ——

HERBS

When we first started to run Kinloch as a hotel,
seventeen years ago, the hardest thing of all to get was
a dependable supply of fresh vegetables and fruit.
There was one wholesaler supplying the island in
those days, and he travelled from Inverness every two
weeks. He would deliver first to the shops and then to
the hotels (those that bothered with fresh vegetables
and fruit in those days – sadly many didn't).

Opposite and above: A rich selection of organic vegetables
grown by Jacki Buchan, who supplies many of the local hotels.

IN THE old days, it was not unusual for our fruit and vegetable order to sit in a lorry for up to three days before it reached us. Three days in a hot lorry in summertime did nothing to improve lettuces, for example, which were limp even before their journey began. And the order was so pathetic anyway. Try as I might – and I did try, very hard, threatening, pleading, cajoling – the wholesalers would not bring me anything as exotic as a mushroom. Even in those days mushrooms were being extensively farmed, and availability to the wholesaler was no problem, but he just couldn't believe that I really wanted them. Our vegetables used to consist of potatoes, carrots, onions, cabbage and turnip, with lettuce and tomatoes in the summer months. That was our first year. By the second year we had established a sort of vegetable garden, with a very eccentric gardener who tended to grow what he wanted rather than what we wanted. When I forced his hand, the results became victim to every known horticultural disease, and several which I'm sure were his own invention. Not being a gardener myself, I had no chance of outwitting him. So we had courgettes till we – and I'm sure our guests – were sick of them, and strawberries. We had iceberg lettuce (which the gardener was very dubious about at first, but of which he became very fond, hence their guaranteed wellbeing and supply), and we had parsley, dill, chives and chervil – he liked the herbs – although we have never been able to grow any variety of mint successfully. We are the only people I know who can't grow mint. Most people grow their mint in buckets to prevent it from spreading like wildfire throughout their garden.

The reason for the lack of a supply of fruit and vegetables to Skye, and to other rural parts of Scotland, was that the Scots had just never had much of a variety of vegetables. They have always eaten potatoes. Indeed, over the centuries potatoes formed a major part of their diet (along with oatmeal, and fish). The only other vegetables eaten throughout Scotland were turnip and onions and, to a lesser extent, cabbage and carrots.

Fruit was equally hard to come by. Godfrey remembers that as a child in Skye he never saw an orange in the shop, nor bananas. Luckily, times have changed. In the shop in Ardvasar, the village ten miles down the road from us, you can buy red, green and yellow peppers, aubergines and avocados. It is almost unbelievable when I remember that, seventeen years ago, the same shop hardly stocked tinned tomatoes, never mind fresh! This recent demand for a greater variety of fruit and vegetables comes from a growing awareness of how what we eat affects our bodies, and a desire to broaden the range of dishes cooked in the home.

Our major supplier of fruit and vegetables now is Norman Macleod, a wholesale and retailer in Portree. His firm buys from the Glasgow Fruit Market twice a week, and he telephones us for our order at the beginning and end of each week. He always warns us if something is unobtainable, so that we can plan in advance. His quality is the best, and as for the variety ... we can buy almost anything these days – limes, for instance, when even lemons used to be a rarity. We get cherries, apricots and celeriac in season. I don't think I shall ever take for granted the variety and dependability of Norman Macleod's deliveries, because I shall never forget the frustrations of our early years in the hotel business, struggling to buy fruit and vegetables which were taken for granted further south. I remember well how in our first year the *Good Food Guide*, while commending us, castigated us for our use of frozen vegetables. In an effort to give our guests some variety from the same old cabbage, carrots and turnip, I used to offer frozen peas and beans etc.

Norman Macleod not only supplies us with most of our fruit and vegetables, but also with our bread flours,

*Above: A sundial nestles in Artemisia at
the herb farm, Scotherbs.
Opposite: Robert Wilson and Stanley Turner of Scotherbs.*

teas, sugar, honey, oatmeals, nuts and dried fruits. Several years ago he expanded his business to include a wide range of health foods, which saved us getting those by mail order from Edinburgh. He also brings us all our wine supplies, so we are heavily dependent on Norman. He is very hardworking and versatile in all his enterprises, which include a haulage business. He is also the undertaker for the island.

We also buy fruit and vegetables from two other excellent sources. Peter Tarry, here in Skye, supplies us with all our strawberries, some early potatoes, lettuce, broad beans and runner beans. Jacki Buchan, at Morar, several miles down the coast from Mallaig, supplies us with a variety of other produce. Jacki is typical of the many enterprising people who have come to live and work here in Scotland. She used to be a primary school teacher in the East End of London until she came to live in Morar six years ago. She had always spent her holidays in Scotland, and when the house in Morar came on the market, with eleven acres of land, she bought it. Much of the eleven acres is boggy, and she is gradually reclaiming it to extend her organic cultivation of fruit and vegetables. She makes her own compost, with local manure, using seaweed to activate it. She learns more about gardening as each year passes – she says she can't afford to make mistakes because a whole year has to pass before she gets a second chance. In spite of the enormous amount of very hard work involved – the digging alone must seem end-

Jacki Buchan grows her organic produce in two tunnels. In this tunnel she cultivates strawberries, asparagus, spring cabbages, tomatoes, aubergines and green peppers.

less – she gets lots of satisfaction out of her new lifestyle, and her problem is not to find enough customers, but to be able to grow enough to supply demand.

Jacki grows her produce in two tunnels. In the number one tunnel she grows strawberries, asparagus, spring cabbages, and tomatoes. Each year she grows a different variety of tomato – the 1989 crop was Ailsa Craig. Also in number one tunnel Jacki grows aubergines, green peppers, French beans and this year, for the first time, Ogen melons. The number two tunnel contains courgettes, red curly lettuce, and several sorts of potato – ratte, desiree, concorde, kondor and romano. She grows everything from seed. As well as Kinloch, Jacki also supplies Inverlochy, Ardsheal and many other hotels and restaurants in her area.

Before people like Peter Tarry and Jacki Buchan came to live and work as market gardeners in Scotland, large houses with walled gardens grew a wide variety of fruits and vegetables. One might think that the uncertain weather in Scotland, especially further north, would preclude the growing of all but the hardiest fruit and vegetables, but this is not the case. At Armadale, Godfrey's former family home here in Skye, there were great glasshouses that used to stretch along the walls of the vast walled garden. These were sited to catch the maximum sunlight, and peaches and grapes used to flourish behind the glass. On one wall, not under glass, I remember a fig tree which produced delicious figs in abundance. But for the most part, the produce for which Scotland is best known is fruit, mostly fruiting in the summer and autumn months. The exception is rhubarb, with early forced rhubarb appearing in gardens throughout Scotland from April onwards, and even earlier, if we have an exceptionally mild spring.

Wild raspberries are the next fruit to be found – they grow in July and August. They must be the most delicious of all fruit, with their intense flavour and jewel-like colour. In a blind tasting of raspberry jam one year at the local WRI (Women's Rural Institute) competition, I could spot the jam made from wild (as opposed to cultivated) raspberries easily – and gave it first prize (and ate half the contents of the pot in the judging). Raspberries are mainly cultivated on Tayside, especially in the area around Blairgowrie.

At Invergowrie, near Dundee, is the Scottish Crop Research Institute, where research goes on continuously

A bowl of chanterelles, my favourites. These can be found in the woods beside Kinloch Lodge.

in the search for soft fruit, especially raspberries, which will last longer yet retain their flavour, and which are less prone to disease. At the Institute raspberries have been crossed with blackberries to produce the Tayberry, a large, firm, strongly flavoured fruit which becomes available in greater quantity each year, as its popularity grows. There are, fortunately, an increasing number of fruit farmers who shun chemical sprays, and people will travel a long way to buy from these farms. There is a growing number of pick-your-own fruit farms throughout Scotland, mostly for raspberries and strawberries. At Kinloch we use raspberries in many different puddings. When they first come into season there is nothing nicer than a plate of raspberries, dusted with caster sugar, and served with thick cream. Once the initial delight of raspberries in season wears off, we make raspberry ice-cream, and serve it with a raspberry sauce – made by liquidizing the raspberries with icing sugar, and sieving the purée to remove the woody pips. Raspberry and lemon sorbet or water ice is refreshing and delicious. Raspberries combine very well with cinnamon, and a cinnamon ice-cream with a raspberry sauce is delicious. Raspberries – and strawberries – go very well with almonds and hazelnuts, and the classic hazelnut meringue can be enhanced by a filling of raspberries and whipped cream and served with raspberry sauce. An old Scottish pudding is Crannachan, where raspberries and cream and curd cheese (crowdie) are mixed together with oatmeal steeped overnight in

whisky and honey. It is very good, providing there isn't too much oatmeal, which can make Crannachan rather a stodgy pudding. If there is a super abundance of raspberries, raspberry jelly (made the same way as bramble jelly) is a positive luxury food, and raspberry jam comes a close second, providing the jam is not overcooked. When it is overboiled, raspberry jam loses its beautiful bright colour and fresh flavour and goes brown as the sugar caramelizes. Raspberries freeze very well, which means that they can be used in winter months to refresh jaded palates with a taste from the summer. One of the most delicious puddings I have ever eaten was at Inverlochy several years ago. It was raspberries underneath a perfect vanilla-flavoured *crème brûlée*. It was so good that I chose it two nights running. However, I would only make this with fresh raspberries, never with frozen fruit.

Strawberries are fruit which I only like to eat in season, and only when grown in this country. Although they are to be found on the shelves of shops virtually all year round, in my opinion they can be pretty tasteless berries, and in the winter months they are grown in far-flung corners of the world. The flavour of organically grown strawberries, such as those we use here, is superb. The flavour of strawberries is greatly enhanced by lemon, orange and elderflower. Strawberries, traditionally, are eaten with cream in Britain, but I prefer to do as the Italians do, and eat them with an acid combination such as lemon or orange, which brings out their taste.

Elderflower, those clusters of tiny cream flowers, grow in our hedges from about the third week in June till the third week in August, depending, as ever, on the weather. I love elderflower, with its exquisite almost muscat grape flavour, and combined with lemon in a syrup it is the perfect marinade for strawberries. Other alternatives are freshly squeezed orange juice with an orange-based liqueur such as Grand Marnier or Cointreau. A delectable pudding is a combination of Vanilla Pavlova, spread with a lemon and elderflower curd, with sliced strawberries scattered thickly over the surface – to which some like to add whipped cream. A meringue made with almonds and filled with sliced strawberries in whipped cream is divine, especially if the top layer of meringue is coated with a coffee glacé icing.

Dramatic skies above the wheat fields on the Black Isle near Muir of Ord, Ross-shire, in the Highlands.

The beautifully laid out herb garden at Scotherbs, near Errol, Perthshire.

This is a classic Cordon Bleu recipe, called Strawberry Japonais. The one thing I loathe in combination with strawberries or raspberries is chocolate. For my taste, the sweetness of the chocolate makes both fruits taste very sour, while the acidity of the fruits kills the flavour of the chocolate. Sadly, strawberries do not freeze well. They turn to mush on thawing.

Brambles, or blackberries, grow thickly and rampantly throughout Scotland. There is something intensely satisfying about bramble picking expeditions, possibly deriving from the fact that the best brambles always seem to grow hanging over ravines, above streams. This means dangling, holding on to bits of rock with the toes of your wellies, in order to stretch for the luscious brambles hanging almost but not quite out of reach. I do resent other people picking brambles within what I consider to be my patches – I become extremely territorial at the bramble picking time! Brambles are in season from the end of August till the first few days of October, but these approximate dates depend very much on the weather. I am such an ardent bramble picker that I remember the date of each year's first picking. The earliest ever in my experience was in 1988, when my first bramble picking expedition was on 6 August. Wild brambles have a wonderful taste, even if they are hazardous and painful to pick – painful, because of the prickles on the stems, which leave your fingers stained with a combination of bramble juice and blood from the inevitable scratches! Cultivated brambles are bigger and altogether tamer fruit, having no prickles, and a flavour that is just not as good as that of their smaller, wild counterparts. Brambles freeze very well, just packed into polythene bags, and they can then be made into winter puddings, such as steamed lemon and bramble pudding, or spiced bramble fudge crumble. As with raspberries, lemon complements the flavour of brambles, and a thick purée of liquidized brambles, sieved and cooked with lemon, makes a delicious sauce to serve with meringues, or with apple pie. Bramble and lemon mousse is another favourite of ours, and so is bramble and lemon *suedoise* – a thick purée of lemon-flavoured brambles, set with gelatine and turned out, covered with whipped cream and studded with tiny meringues. And, of course, bramble jelly is wonderful, especially served with warm oven scones or pancakes.

Rowan berries appear on the trees in September (or late August) and last through to the first days of November, unless the weather is exceptionally wet, when the berries tend to shrivel on their twigs. Rowan trees are thought to have supernatural powers. The author Gavin Maxwell who, until his death, lived on the mainland opposite Skye, blamed all his misfortunes, leading up to his death, on being cursed under a rowan tree. I wish I knew how this superstition originated. But rowan (in Scotland the -ow- is pronounced as in ouch) provide jewel-like colour in the autumn months, and the berries make a bitter jelly which is the perfect accompaniment for rich game meats of all types. If you taste rowan jelly by itself, don't be put off by its undeniable bitterness, because when eaten with roast grouse, for example, or with venison, it comes into its own. I like to put Cox's apples in my rowan jelly – cooking apples have altogether too tart a flavour. Sometimes I add a stick of cinnamon to the fruit for the jelly as it cooks, giving a faintly spicy tang to the jelly, which I like, especially with roast pheasant.

One of the richest crops growing wild throughout the Scottish countryside are the mushrooms and fungi. The quantity of wild mushrooms varies from year to year, but they always grow in the same places, and seem to grow overnight between one picking to the next. One year they will grow in abundance, the next there will scarcely be a wild mushroom to be found. One memorable year Godfrey picked 28 pounds in a single day! That was about twelve years ago, and we have never had a year like it since. However, our woods are always thick with edible fungi, of a wide variety. The very word fungi is so repulsive and off-putting that it is far more appealing when writing menus and recipes to refer to them inaccurately as wild mushrooms. Both Godfrey and my son Hugo are fanatical mushroom and fungi pickers – and eaters. Hugo must be the only boy in his class to eat horns of plenty sautéed in olive oil with garlic for breakfast before he catches the school bus! My favourites are chanterelles. They are a bright orangey yellow colour, with fluted gills. They are quite unmistakable, once you know what to look for, and they are to be found in mossy terrain underneath trees, particularly beech trees. Other great favourites which grow in woods right beside our house are the dark purplish black horns of plenty, whose trumpets go right down their stems. We have ceps of many varieties – they are not my favourite, although many do prize them. They have spongy underneaths, which are too often homes for maggots, and this is what has put me off them over the years! Hedgehog mushrooms taste delicious – they are a pale creamy yellow and have a prickly appearance underneath, where other species usually have gills. Wild fungi are still viewed with suspicion by many people in Scotland, but there are a growing number of enthusiasts like ourselves, who fully realize the value of the delicacies growing free for the picking all around us, and for which people in cities pay dearly in delicatessens. But to the would-be enthusiast I would say that a well-illustrated book is vital, and the best we have (and we have several) is *Mushrooms and Other Fungi of Great Britain and Europe*, by Roger Philips.

We use wild mushrooms (fungi) as a substitute for the cultivated mushrooms when they are available. We have picked our first chanterelles as early as the end of June, and depending on the weather they go on until late September. A delicious soup is made from chanterelles and leeks, and a combination of wild mushrooms in a creamy sauce makes a good filling for brioches in the autumn as a first course. But best of all I love a simple supper of mixed wild fungi or mushrooms, sautéed in olive oil with garlic and eaten with granary toast.

Two years ago we gave up trying to grow applemint, along with our other herbs, and started to get our herbs by post each week from Scotherbs. Based at the enchantingly named Waterybutts, near Errol in Perthshire, Scotherbs is run by two couples, the Wilsons and the Turners, in the farm buildings where Mr Wilson used to keep his dairy herd. Stanley Turner lives some twenty miles away in Carnoustie. Before embarking on his second career, he was on the staff of Dundee University. He had always loved gardening, and the four friends started their now thriving business six years ago. Sue Turner is a very keen cook, and now runs excellent cooking demonstrations from March to November at Waterybutts, and there is a farmhouse restaurant there, too. Scotherbs supply some fifty hotels and restaurants throughout Scotland with their weekly herb orders, as well as a number of delicatessens.

To have an abundance of herbs is essential. I find we use herbs more and more lavishly in our cooking. I chop basil into prawn and tomato salads, use it to accompany spinach and garlic, or avocado and tomato terrines, and strew chopped basil over tomato tarts and put it into tomato sauces. A great favourite of mine is dill, which goes into all things fishy, and is also delicious in potato concoctions. Other herbs we get include chives, parsley, tarragon and chervil, each beautifully packaged in tough polythene envelopes.

So, thankfully, the scene as regards fresh fruit and vegetables in Scotland has changed dramatically for the better in the last sixteen years. This is reflected in how people who live in Scotland now wish to eat, and how visitors to Scotland expect to eat. And it's so very much better for us all.

Culinary, aromatic, medicinal and decorative herbs are all grown at Scotherbs who supply some fifty hotels and restaurants.

RHUBARB AND GINGER SUEDOISE WITH GINGER MERINGUES

This is a set purée of ginger-flavoured rhubarb – the combined flavours of ginger and rhubarb complement each other perfectly. The rhubarb and ginger 'jelly' is turned out of its bowl or mould, covered with whipped cream and decorated with small ginger meringues.

Serves 8

2 sachets / US 4 envelopes unflavoured gelatine powder (1oz/25g)
2lb/ 900g rhubarb,
cut into 2 inch / 5cm chunks
1 pint / 2½ cups / 600ml water
6oz / 1¼ cups / 175g soft brown sugar
6 pieces preserved ginger, drained of syrup and chopped quite finely
¾ pint / 2 cups / 450ml double (heavy) cream

Ginger meringues

3 egg whites
6oz / ¾ cup / 175g caster (superfine) sugar
1 tsp ground ginger

Sprinkle the gelatine over 4 tbsp cold water and leave to soak. Put the prepared rhubarb into the saucepan together with the water and sugar. Over a moderate heat, stir to dissolve the sugar, then cook the rhubarb until it begins to fall apart. Stir the gelatine and water mixture into the hot rhubarb and continue stirring for 2–3 minutes to let the gelatine dissolve completely. Liquidize the rhubarb mixture, whizzing until the purée is smooth and not at all fibrous. If your liquidizer has rather blunt blades and can't cope with the rhubarb fibres, sieve the purée, to get a really smooth texture. Stir the chopped preserved ginger through the purée, and pour into a 3 pint / 2 quart / 1·75 litre bowl. Leave to set in the refrigerator for several hours, or overnight.

To make the meringues, line two bak-ing sheets with baking parchment. In a bowl, whisk the egg whites until they are very stiff, then whisk in the sugar a spoonful at a time and continue whisking until the meringue is very stiff. Sift the ginger over the meringue and, with a large metal spoon, fold the ginger through the meringue quickly and thoroughly.

Spoon the mixture into a piping (pastry) bag and pipe, using a star-shaped nozzle, into rounds the size of a 10p bit (50c piece) on the lined baking sheets. Bake in a preheated very cool oven (250°F / 130°C / gas ½) for 2–2½ hours, or until the meringues are firm and will lift cleanly off the baking parchment. Cool them on a wire rack, and when cold store them in an airtight container.

To turn out the suedoise, dip the bowl into hot water for several seconds, invert a serving plate over the bowl, turn the right way up and give a good shake; if the suedoise doesn't come out of the bowl, just repeat the hot water dipping process for a few more seconds.

Whip the cream until fairly stiff, and spread over the surface of the suedoise. Stick the meringues on to the cream, all over the suedoise. Serve as soon as possible.

STRAWBERRIES IN LEMON AND ELDERFLOWER SYRUP

Lemon and elderflower taste exquisite together, and they bring out the flavour of strawberries wonderfully well. Elderflower blooms in the hedgerows and gardens from mid-June to the end of July in Scotland.

Serves 6

1½ pints / 3¾ cups / 900ml cold water
6oz / ¾ cup / 175g sugar
2 handfuls of elderflowers
pared rind and juice of 2 lemons
2lb / about 3 pints / 900g strawberries, hulled and sliced

Measure the water into a saucepan and add the sugar and lemon rind. Over a moderate heat, stir until the sugar has completely dissolved, then bring to the boil and boil the syrup fast for 5 minutes, with the pan uncovered. Draw the pan off the heat, and plunge the elderflowers and lemon juice into the hot syrup. When the syrup is quite cold, strain it into a serving bowl. Stir the strawberries gently into the syrup and leave to marinate for several hours before serving.

STEAMED LEMON AND BRAMBLE PUDDING

People love an old-fashioned steamed pudding, and this one is very easy and quick to make. It is even easier if you have a boilable plastic pudding basin with a snap-on lid.

Serves 6–8

1½lb / 5 cups / 700g brambles (blackberries)
3oz / ⅔ cup / 90g soft brown sugar
10oz / 2 cups / 300g plain (all-purpose) flour
3oz / 6 tbsp / 90g caster (US granulated) sugar
1½ tsp bicarbonate of soda (baking soda)
4oz / 120g shredded suet, either beef suet or vegetarian suet
grated rind and juice of 2 lemons
2 size 2 / US extra large eggs, beaten
¼ pint / ⅔ cup / 150ml milk

In the bottom of a 3 pint / 2 quart / 1·75 litre pudding basin (or steaming mold), mix together the brambles and brown sugar. Sift the flour, caster (US granulated) sugar and soda into a mixing bowl. Stir in the suet, and beat in the grated lemon rind and juice, the eggs and milk. Beat all well together, then pour the mixture into the pudding basin on top of the brambles.

Opposite: the imposing architecture of St. Andrew's Square, Edinburgh.

Cover with a disc of greaseproof paper (baking parchment) and snap on the lid or cover with foil tied on with string. Put the basin into a saucepan of boiling water that will come halfway up the sides of the basin. Cover the pan with a lid. Steam the pudding, with the water simmering gently around the basin, for 2–2½ hours. Remember to top up the water in the saucepan from time to time.

The pudding can be kept warm after the cooking time is up by just sitting in the water in the pan. To serve, turn out on to a serving plate.

Toasted Coconut and Vanilla Ice-Cream with Raspberry and Cinnamon Sauce

These flavours – the toasted coconut, vanilla, raspberry and cinnamon – go together very well indeed, and this makes a delicious summertime dessert.

Serves 8

¾ pint / 2 cups / 450ml double (heavy) cream
6 eggs, separated
1 tsp vanilla essence (extract)
6oz / 1½ cups / 175g icing (confectioners')sugar
4oz / 1 cup / 120g desiccated (dried shredded) coconut, toasted till pale golden and cooled

Sauce

1lb / 2 pints / 450g raspberries
2–3oz / ½–¾ cup / 60–90g icing (confectioners') sugar
2 tsp ground cinnamon

To make the ice-cream, whip the cream until it is fairly thick, then whip in the egg yolks and vanilla. In a large bowl, whisk the egg whites until stiff, then whisk in the sifted icing (confectioners') sugar a spoonful at a time and continue whisking until the

A selection of puddings served at Kinloch Lodge including blackcurrant bavarois with blackcurrant and cassis coulis, and rhubarb and ginger suedoise with ginger meringues.

meringue is stiff. Fold the toasted coconut into the cream mixture, then fold in the meringue. Freeze.

For the sauce, liquidize the raspberries with the sugar and cinnamon, then sieve the resulting purée – no blades will break down the little woody raspberry pips.

Take the ice-cream out of the freezer and leave at room temperature for half an hour before serving, with the sauce.

Raspberry and Lemon Water Ice

This water ice has a lemon-based syrup which really enhances the flavour of the raspberries. The more times it is beaten in a food processor during the freezing process, the softer and lighter it will be.

Serves 8

1½ pints / 3¾ cups / 900ml water
10oz / 1¼ cups / 300g sugar
pared rind and juice of 3 lemons
1½lb / 3 pints / 700g raspberries, liquidized into a purée then sieved

Put the water, sugar and lemon rind in a saucepan over a moderate heat, and stir to dissolve the sugar. When the sugar has completely dissolved (but not before), boil the syrup fast for 7–10 minutes. Then take the pan off the heat and stir in the lemon juice.

When the syrup has cooled, fish out the bits of lemon rind and stir together the raspberry purée and syrup. Pour into a shallow container and freeze for several hours.

When it is fairly well solid, take the container out of the freezer, scoop the contents into a food processor and whiz until the mixture is mushy. Refreeze, and repeat the whizzing and refreezing as often as you can – a minimum of three times. If you do this, the water ice will increase in volume and you will be able to serve it straight from the freezer.

BLACKCURRANT BAVAROIS WITH BLACKCURRANT AND CASSIS COULIS

Quite apart from the attractive colour contrast between the paler creamy bavarois and its accompanying darker sauce, or coulis, this dessert is convenient in that it is made completely in advance, and the blackcurrants don't need to be topped and tailed. I like to set it in a loaf tin or terrine, and then turn it out and cut it in slices about 1 inch / 2·5cm thick.

Serves 8

Bavarois

1½lb / 5 cups / 700g fresh blackcurrants
juice of ½ lemon
1 sachet / 2 US envelopes unflavoured
gelatine powder (½oz / 15g)
3 tbsp cold water
½ pint / 1¼ cups / 300ml single (light)
cream
3 size 2 / US extra large egg yolks
4oz / ½ cup / 120g caster
(US granulated) sugar
½ pint / 1¼ cup / 300ml double (heavy)
cream, whipped but not stiffly

Coulis

1lb / 3 cups / 450g fresh blackcurrants
1 pint / 2½ cups / 600ml water
3oz / 6tbsp / 90g sugar
4 tbsp crème de cassis
(blackcurrant liqueur)

Put the blackcurrants into a saucepan with the lemon juice. Cover the pan with a lid, and cook the currants over moderate heat until the juices run from the fruit. Take the currants off the heat and purée them in a blender or food processor, then rub

through a sieve to remove all the pips and other debris.

Sprinkle the gelatine over the cold water and leave until spongy.

Meanwhile, heat the single (light) cream until it just forms a skin. In a bowl, beat together the egg yolks and sugar, then pour on a little of the hot cream. Mix well and pour into the saucepan with the rest of the cream. Over a low heat, and stirring all the time with a wooden spoon, cook this custard until it is thick enough to coat the back of the wooden spoon. This will take several minutes – anything up to 10 – but it must not be hurried because it could curdle if it gets too hot.

When the custard has thickened, add the gelatine mixture and stir until the gelatine dissolves completely in the hot custard. Lastly, fold in the sieved blackcurrant purée. Leave to cool completely.

When the blackcurrant mixture is quite cold, fold in the whipped cream. Pour into a 2lb / 1kg or 9 x 5 x 3 inch / 23 x 12·5 x 7·5cm loaf tin or terrine. Cover and leave in the refrigerator to set – overnight if possible.

To make the coulis, put the blackcurrants, water and sugar into a pan, and heat until the sugar dissolves and the currants soften. Purée in a blender or food processor, then rub through a sieve. Stir the cassis into the sauce. Taste for sweetness, and add more sugar if you like in the form of icing (confectioners') sugar, which will dissolve much more easily than a grainier sugar.

Serve the coulis spooned beside or over the slices of bavarois.

LEMON AND ELDERFLOWER CURD

This recipe has appeared in three of my books already, but I make no apology for including it in this book, too. Scotland is full of elderflower bushes, and I love to make the most of them whilst they are in flower, from about mid-June to the end of July,

although last year I picked my last cluster of elderflower, unbelievably, on August 19th.

Makes about 2lb / 900g

12oz / 1½ cups / 350g caster
(US granulated) sugar
6oz / 1½ sticks / 175g butter
finely grated rind and juice of 4 lemons
3 handfuls of elderflowers
3 size 2 / US extra large eggs
3 egg yolks

Into a heatproof bowl put the sugar, butter cut into bits, the grated lemon rind and juice and the elderflowers, plucked from their stalks. In another bowl, beat together the whole eggs and yolks, then strain these into the bowl containing the other ingredients.

Put the bowl over a saucepan of barely simmering water, on a moderate heat. With a wire whisk, stir the lemony mixture until the butter melts and the sugar dissolves completely. After this stage there really is no need to stir the mixture constantly, but give it a stir from time to time as the curd thickens. When it is thick, take the bowl off the heat, and pot the curd into warm jars.

Let the curd cool completely before sealing the jars, and store them in the refrigerator.

ROWAN AND APPLE JELLY

Rowan jelly can be awfully bitter, which is why I put apples in mine. I also like to add a cinnamon stick, to give a subtle and barely discernible hint of spice to the jelly.

Makes about 6lbs / 2·8kg

2lb / 900g rowan berries
2lb / 900g eating apples – any sort
except Golden Delicious, which are
tasteless – quartered
4 pints / 2½ quarts / 2·5 litres water
1 cinnamon stick
2lb / 4 cups / 900g sugar

Into a large saucepan, put the rowan berries, quartered apples, water and cinnamon stick. Bring the water to a simmer and cook, with the pan half covered, for 35–40 minutes or until the berries can be squashed against the sides of the pan with the back of your wooden spoon and the pieces of apple are soft. Strain the liquid from the cooked fruit through a jelly bag (or muslin or cheesecloth) into a bowl. Don't be tempted to squeeze the contents of the jelly bag; just let it drip for several hours, until all the liquid has dripped through.

Put the liquid from the bowl into a clean saucepan and add the sugar. Over a moderate heat stir to dissolve the sugar completely, then let the liquid boil fast for 10–15 minutes before testing for a set: remove the pan from the heat, drip some of the jelly on to a saucer and leave for a few minutes to cool, then push the surface with your finger. If it wrinkles, you have a set. If it doesn't wrinkle, boil up the liquid fast for a further 5 minutes before testing for a set once more.

Pot into warmed jars and seal. Label the jars and store them in a cool place.

SPICED BRAMBLE FUDGE CRUMBLE

This is a perfect pudding for the family. Cinnamon complements all berried fruit, especially brambles. Fudge crumble is very good with vanilla ice cream or with thick Greek-style yoghurt.

Serves 6–8

2lb / about 3 pints / 900g brambles
(blackberries)
1 cinnamon stick
3oz / $\frac{2}{3}$ cup / 90g soft brown sugar

Crumble

10–12 digestive biscuits
(graham cracker halves)
5oz / 1$\frac{1}{4}$ sticks / 150g butter
5oz / 1 cup / 150g demerara
(raw brown) sugar

Rowan and apple jelly as served at Kinloch Lodge.

Put the brambles, cinnamon stick and sugar into a saucepan with a tightly fitting lid. Over a gentle-to-moderate heat, cook the brambles until the juices run – there is no need to add water as the berries make their own juice. Once the brambles are cooked, take the pan off the heat and leave to cool. When cold, fish out the cinnamon stick and pour the brambles into an ovenproof dish.

To make the crumble, put the digestive biscuits (graham crackers) into a food processor and whiz until they are fine crumbs. Melt the butter in a saucepan and add the demerara (raw brown) sugar and crumbs. Stir well then spoon this mixture evenly over the brambles.

Bake in a preheated hot oven (425°F/220°C/gas 7) for 15–30 minutes – until the crumble is firm on top. Serve warm.

LEEK, MUSHROOM AND CHANTERELLE SOUP

Quite apart from combining delicious flavours, this is an excellent soup to start an otherwise rich dinner. It is also a boon to those who, like me, are always counting calories! This soup is as good as the stock used in its making. I am a passionate maker of stock, and consider that really good soup must be based on a home-made stock, whether it is chicken, game, beef, vegetable stock or whatever. The awful stock cubes just won't do. If you are not lucky enough to have ready access to an abundance of chanterelles, just leave them out of the recipe and double the quantity of mushrooms.

Serves 8

2oz / 4 tbsp / 60g butter
1 onion, peeled and chopped
3 medium-sized leeks, finely sliced
8oz / 225g mushrooms, chopped
8oz / 225g chanterelles, chopped
2 pints / 5 cups / 1·25 litres good
chicken or vegetable stock
salt and freshly ground pepper
1 tbsp finely chopped parsley

Melt the butter in a saucepan, add the chopped onion and cook until the onion is soft and translucent. Then add the leeks and cook for a further 5 minutes. Add the chopped mushrooms and chanterelles and cook for a minute or two with the leeks and onion, then pour in the stock. Simmer very gently for 15 minutes.

Season to taste with salt and pepper and, just before serving, stir the parsley through the soup.

MUSSEL, ONION AND PARSLEY SOUP

Mussels grow on rocks all around Scotland's shores, but they grow in abundance in suspect places like sewage outlets. So do be careful where you pick them. On the other hand, mussels are farmed in Scotland, growing up ropes, and it is generally much safer to buy these farmed mussels unless you are sure of the harvesting ground where you pick from. If you do pick your own, put them in a bucket of water with a couple of handsful of oatmeal; theoretically, the mussels clean themselves in the oatmealy water. Mussels and onions go together so well, and this is an elegant soup as well as being delicious.

Serves 8

2–3 pints / US 2½–3½ pints / 1·25–1·75
litres mussels, well scrubbed under cold
running water
1½ pints / 3¾ cups / 900ml water
½ pint / 1¼ cups / 300ml dry white wine
1 onion, peeled and halved
2oz / 4 tbsp / 60g butter
3 onions, peeled and chopped
2 potatoes, peeled and finely chopped
freshly ground black pepper
freshly grated nutmeg
2 tbsp finely chopped parsley

Put the mussels into a large saucepan with the water, white wine and halved onion. Cover the pan tightly with a lid, and put the pan over high heat. When the liquid has come to a boil cook for about 10 minutes or until the mussels open, then remove from the heat. Discard any that don't open as this means they were dead when picked. Strain off and reserve the cooking liquor.

Melt the butter in a clean saucepan, add the chopped onions and potatoes and cook for 5–7 minutes. Pour in the reserved cooking liquor and simmer gently until the pieces of potato are soft. Liquidize the soup, and return to the pan. Season to taste with pepper and nutmeg.

A sustaining bowl of mussel, onion and parsley soup.

While the soup is cooking, shell the opened mussels. Add them to the liquidized soup and reheat briefly. Just before serving, stir the parsley through soup.

CARROT, TURNIP AND LENTIL SOUP

The Scots are renowned for their soups, and this one is marvellous for cold winter days or evenings as it is thick and satisfying. I like to serve it with warm granary bread as an accompaniment.

Serves 8

2oz / 4 tbsp / 60g butter
2 onions, peeled and chopped
4 carrots, peeled and chopped
½ medium-sized turnip,
peeled and chopped
4oz / ½ cup / 120g orange lentils
2 pints / 5 cups / 1·25 litres good
chicken or vegetable stock
1 large garlic clove, peeled and chopped
salt and freshly ground black pepper
1–2 tbsp finely chopped parsley

Melt the butter in a saucepan, add the chopped onions and cook until the onions are soft and translucent. Add the chopped carrots, turnip and lentils and stir well into the onions, then pour in the stock. Half cover the pan with a lid, and simmer the soup gently for 35–40 minutes. Halfway through the simmering, add the chopped garlic. (If you add it at the beginning along with the other vegetables, you won't notice its presence in the soup – the longer garlic is cooked the less predominant its taste.)

Take the pan off the heat and cool a bit, then liquidize the soup. Pour the smooth soup into a clean saucepan and reheat. Season to taste with salt and pepper. Just before serving, stir the parsley through the soup, but leave this until the very last minute because the parsley will lose its bright fresh colour and taste if it sits in the hot soup for any length of time.

The Grain

—— AND THE ——

Grape

For those who like to drink whisky but know little about its origins, the place to visit is the Whisky Centre in Aviemore. It was the brainchild of Frank Clark, who thought of the idea while he was running the Aberlour Hotel and selling a wide variety of whiskies to people who were continually asking about its history. Frank, I believe, knows more than anyone else in Scotland about whisky, and he is much in demand to lecture on it. He has the knack of being able to convey a great deal of knowledge in a fascinating and amusing way.

Opposite: Frank Clark of the Whisky Centre, Aviemore.
Above: A selection of fine single malt whiskies.

HERE IN Scotland we were late starters in the art of distilling. It is generally thought that missionaries first introduced it to Scotland – they were distilling in Ireland in the thirteenth century, and it came to Scotland about 150 years later. The Irish say that the art of distilling was a gift of St Patrick. The first people to use barley were the Egyptians, and the Moors spread the technique into Europe, where they learnt to distil wine into a form of brandy. But in spite of Scotland's comparatively late start in the use of distilling, we now have a product unequalled by anyone else, and Scotch whisky is better known world-wide than any other national drink – with the possible exception of Coca-Cola! Whisky is a very major Scottish industry – not as big as oil, but definitely of considerable importance to our economy.

In 1860 in France a disease called Philoxera wiped out the Cognac grape production and the English turned to whisky instead, but they found the Highland whisky too strong a taste, and so blended whisky came into being. Blended whiskies now account for 97% of all whisky sold at home and abroad. The variety of blends is bewildering – there are three thousand registered names, although that number includes labels such as that of the Scots Guards, for example, who have their own blend. Although blends vary in flavour, there is nothing like the variation between single malts. A de-luxe blend is older than standard and has a higher percentage of malt whisky, making for a richer flavour and a more mellow whisky. Examples of de-luxe blends are Chivas Regal, Johnny Walker Black Label and Dimple Haig.

Today more and more people are turning to single malt whisky, especially as an after dinner drink. Single malt is the product of an individual malt distillery, and is unmixed with anything else. There are now over seventy distilleries bottling single malts, each one with its own particular characteristics and flavours, although each dis-

Scotland has always been famous for whisky but today many Scottish hotels and restaurants have outstanding wine cellars.

tillery basically uses the same process. There are many things that make for the differing flavours, for example the malting of the barley, and the amount of peat smoke used. Islay distillers use more, giving their whisky a more pungent flavour. In Spey they don't use it, or use very little, and in Orkney they use burnt heather in the drying process. The water that they use to make the whisky in Islay is peaty water, whereas Spey whisky is made from water from granite and peat, which makes the whiskies from Spey less heavy than the Islay malts. Each distillery has its own water supply and won't deviate from it, so distilleries have different mineral contents in their water. During distillation various things affect flavour, such as the way the still is heated – whether by direct flame or by steam coil. The shape of the still is perhaps the most important cause of variations in flavour, as this determines which of the impurities escape over into the condenser and become part of the whisky.

Copper is a tremendous conductor of heat, and stills can't be made out of anything else. If a still wears out, the new one will be made to exactly the same dimensions, even down to dents in the same places!

At the end of distillation there is left a colourless liquid, high in alcohol. At this stage it has to go through a stage of maturation in oak casks. All Scotch whisky must be at least three years old to qualify being called Scotch whisky, so both grain and malt whisky have been lying dormant for over three years. Nearly all single malts bottles are labelled with the ages. Most malts vary in age from eight to fifteen years, although there are some considerably older. While the whisky is maturing in the casks it is breathing through the wood – oxydizing and breaking down some of the harsher impurities, while taking in flavour from the oak cask. Some distilleries use sherry casks for the maturation, which gives a richer colour and flavour. Because the whisky is colourless when it goes into the

Previous page: The River Dee near Ballater.
Above: Two rare vintage single malts.

cask, it gets its colour from the cask as it matures. There is considerable evaporation during maturation – a twelve-year-old whisky loses 20% as it matures, so evaporation takes place at the rate of between 1½% and 2% a year.

After the Act of Union, in 1707, the Scots started to have imposed on them all sorts of laws which made legal whisky production prohibitively expensive. At the end of the eighteenth century the Glenlivet area was renowned for its whisky production. The name appeared in court circulars, and was even mentioned in ministers' diaries. The reason Glenlivet prospered was that it was – still is – a very isolated area, and whisky making could take place there undisturbed by visits from the excise officers, or gaugers, as they were then known. In 1823 the laws were reformed in order to stamp out illegal distilling. Because

the name Glenlivet was already well known, virtually all distilleries used the same name when they went into legal production. It wasn't until 1880, when J. and G. Smith took out legal proceedings against a number of distillers, that court ruled that only Minmore (the Smiths' distillery) could use the name The Glenlivet, but that anyone else could use the word Glenlivet as a suffix, providing it was hyphenated and the size of lettering in the word Glenlivet was not larger than the letters in the name of the actual distillery. As a result there are still many distilleries using the word Glenlivet: hence Dufftown Glenlivet, Tormore Glenlivet and Longmorn Glenlivet, to name a few. The state of the whisky industry now is very buoyant. There is a greater variety of flavours in malt whisky than in any other spirit, and it is impossible to grade them or say which is the best – it is purely a matter of personal taste.

Although you can read books on the subject, the only way of really discovering the delights of whiskies is to try each one. And as Frank Clark says, from his excellent and informative Whisky Centre where he stocks virtually the lot, by the time you have tried them all you will have to start again, because you may well have forgotten the first ones you tasted!

WINE

There are many excellent wine merchants in Scotland, the most northerly being The Wine Shop in Thurso, but the most Scottish of them all must surely be Irvine Robertson Wines, in 'Leith sur Mer', Edinburgh. The firm was started in 1984 by Sandy Irvine Robertson, one of the kindest, most colourful and flamboyant personalities in Scotland today – loved by most, loathed by a very few. Until the birth of Irvine Robertson Wines, Sandy worked for the renowned firm of Justerini and Brooks, and was very well known to all in the hotel and restaurant trade as an enthusiastic wine salesman, travelling the length and breadth of the mainland and the islands, visiting his clients two or three times a year, and dispensing fun, havoc, largesse and a verbal shot in the arm wherever he went. Already a friend of ours long before we embarked on our hotel career – or, to be more accurate, our hotel way of life – Sandy was no less attentive to the needs of people he scarcely knew. And Sandy makes friends with all he meets, with the occasional exception. There are those who, understandably, do not instantly take to Sandy's eccentric exuberance and the forms this can take, but they usually come round to him in the end, once the initial shock has worn off! Sandy is indeed an out-and-out extrovert, but also manages to bring together people who can benefit from each other's acquaintance. We have personal experience of this, because it was Sandy who introduced us to Trevor Knowles, the cheese specialist, when he was embarking on his career, and we became Trevor's first hotel clients.

For all his eccentricities, Sandy is fast establishing Irvine Robertson Wines as one of the foremost wine merchants in Scotland today. Leith is an ideal spot for his base, on account of its longstanding connection with wine. Since the twelfth century Leith has been the centre of the wine trade in Scotland. The walls of its vaults sparkle with a growth of spoor seen elsewhere only in the vaults in Bordeaux. The vaults in Leith were used by the monks of Holyrood, and there is supposed to be a passage leading directly from the vaults to Holyrood. The earliest surviving record of wine in Scotland dates from AD 1, when Roman galleys brought wine to Leith. Another early link with France is to be found in Bordeaux's Musée de Lapidaire, where there is a tomb of a Scottish wine merchant, dated AD 10.

The uniqueness of Irvine Robertson Wines lies in the fact that Sandy is always on the look-out for wine sellers with a Scottish connection to do business with, providing the wines come out top in blind tastings – the wines are not chosen purely because they are produced by people with Scottish ancestry! But an example of this preference for wine producers with Scottish links is that Sandy buys from Penfolds, in Australia, where fine wines are being produced by Ian Mackley, who was born and brought up in Glasgow. Sandy buys Madeira from Cossart Gordon and Co. Ltd, another great name in the wine trade, of Scottish descent. James Gordon, 6th Laird of Letterfourie, in Banffshire, went to Madeira in 1742 and set up a wine business. (His younger brother Alexander served as a volunteer in Bonnie Prince Charlie's Life Guards and fought at Culloden.) Sandy buys port from John Graham, a kinsman of the Duke of Montrose, who established Churchill Graham in 1981, and whose port is producing impressive write-ups from leading wine writers (in publications such as *Decanter*, *The Sunday*

Just a few of the outstanding wines on offer at Cringletie Hotel in the Borders.

Times, *The Standard*, *Harpers Wine* and *Spirit Gazette*).

One of the most popular wines on our list is the 1981 Château Musar Rouge, made by a man called Serge Hochar, who has no Scottish antecedents but who produces wines (and ships them out), against all odds, from Ghazir, some 16 miles north of Beirut. Another favourite stocked by Sandy is a wonderful sweet white wine from Romania, rich and luscious, and unbelievably low priced. It comes from the Dealul Mare region, to the north of Bucharest, and is produced from the Tamiioasa (Frankincense) grape.

Sandy launched his Leith Portfolio wines on the Wogan Show in 1985 at the Edinburgh Festival. This was a memorable show, in which Sandy managed to upstage Wogan in no uncertain way, and to perplex his

Above: The Cragganmore distillery on Speyside and (right) their special still complete with the manufacturer's plaque.

fellow guest, the actor Tom Conti, by confusing him with the boxer John Conteh! The Leith Portfolio consists of Leith Claret, Leith Red Burgundy and Leith White Bordeaux, these three being the Irvine Robertson house wines.

Sandy feels that wines in favour tend to rotate between countries – 1988 was Australia's year, 1989 Chile. His prediction for 1990 was that Italian wines would come to the fore – a view shared by Philip Contini of Valvona and Crolla.

Once a year Irvine Robertson Wines host a splendid wine tasting, at Prestonfield House, on the outskirts of Edinburgh, specifically for trade buyers, restaurateurs and hoteliers like ourselves. The tasting is followed by an extremely good lunch, and it is a day of great interest and fun, as well as a chance to see and talk to other friends in the hotel way of life. Nick Parsons, from Polmaily House Hotel, says that Sandy is easily the best deliverer of his wines, quicker and more reliable than other wine companies, and we whole-heartedly agree. For people like us, running a business off the beaten track, rely very much on our suppliers, and the speed and efficiency with which Sandy's firm delivers our orders typify the very personal service that Irvine Robertson Wines provides.

TRADITIONAL BAKING

Scots baking is welcoming food. An invitation to someone's home guarantees a plate of buttered scones or pancakes, a good cake, and other delectable squares and fingers of rich iced biscuits or cake-based items – all irresistible, and all sadly heavy on the calories, not to mention the cholesterol! But once in a while a splurge is surely permitted. A 'cuppy' (cup of tea) never goes unaccompanied by some form of baking.

Opposite: The cast iron range at Joan Spicer's
Laigh Bakehouse in Hanover Street, Edinburgh.

SCOTTISH BAKING is not the fine patisserie of France and Italy, but more homely and robust. As in France and Italy, many recipes originated in a particular region or town. Take Selkirk bannoch, for example, a rich fruity yeast bread made in a large cob shape, glazed, and served sliced and buttered or, even better, toasted and then buttered. Border tarts, Dundee cake and Aberdeen rowies are other examples of recipes associated with a region or town.

Border tarts are shallow pastry flans with a rich fruit filling and sometimes glacé icing. Dundee cake is a fruit cake covered with circles of split almonds, which toast as the cake cooks, imparting a wonderful flavour to the cake. Aberdeen rowies (also known as butteries, a very descriptive name) are flat buns, deliciously flaky and buttery, made with a dense, salty pastry dough. Good rowies, or butteries, knock spots off the best croissants.

Sometimes a recipe varies in different parts of the country. Take oatcakes, for example. As Catherine Brown says in her excellent book *Scottish Cookery*, the Hebridean oatcake is usually made with fairly fine oatmeal and rolled out to a thickness of between a quarter-inch and a half-inch, making it much thicker and more substantial than the oatcakes made in other regions of Scotland. Oatcakes are wonderful food. Traditionally they were made with bacon fat, and were cooked on a flat iron plate known as a 'girdle', which made them curl upwards. My oatcakes are not traditional as I oven-bake them, and I use butter, and coarse oatmeal – pinhead oatmeal – because I like the chunkier texture which this produces.

Probably the best-known example of traditional Scots baking is shortbread. Recipes for shortbread vary – some people include cornflour in their recipes, some use ground rice or semolina, but basically shortbread is a buttery, crisp pastry, traditionally an inch thick, and cooked in a slow oven. It takes about an hour for short-

Above: A luxurious tea-time spread at Airds Hotel. Opposite: my rich fruit cake the recipe for which is on page 24.

bread to reach the pale golden colour which cooked shortbread should be. As soon as it comes out of the oven it is dusted thickly with caster sugar, so that the sugar sticks to the hot surface. It is then cut into squares or rectangular shapes or, if made in a round tin, into wedges known traditionally as petticoat tails.

There are firms throughout Scotland making excellent shortbread, but the best known must be Walkers of Aberlour, winners of a Queen's Award to Industry, and a firm renowned for their many excellent baked products. Walkers make thick shortbread biscuits with demerara sugar pressed round their edges, called Highlanders. They have recently started to make a chocolate chip shortbread biscuit – just one example of adapting a traditional Scots recipe to make a delicious variation for the present day. Visitors to Scotland buy shortbread in tins to take home. It does make a wonderful present, being typically Scottish and yet able to travel well.

Most households in Scotland have their own recipe for pancakes (drop scones, to those living south of the border), and here, too, there are variations on the basic recipe. I sometimes make pancakes with grated apple in the batter, and I serve them with a cinnamon and sugar butter. Treacle pancakes are good at any time of the year, but are traditionally associated with Hallowe'en.

Oven scones are essentially Scottish, so much so that we make them each morning for our guests' breakfasts. There are many recipes for scones, too, but my favourite is the one we use, which contains golden syrup. For tea-time scone eating I like to make cheese scones – delicious with raspberry jam – or fruit scones, adding raisins or sultanas to the dough.

I have mentioned that treacle pancakes are eaten at Hallowe'en. Another traditional example of Scottish baking which is associated with a particular time of year is Black Bun, a rich fruit cake encased in short pastry and

eaten at New Year. It used to be made with a bread dough encasing the fruit cake, but this was superseded by shortcrust pastry. Whichever is used, I personally find the combination of pastry and fruitcake too much, even for me, but when you consider that Scots housewives traditionally clean their house from top to bottom on New Year's Eve (or used to – here's one that doesn't!), I reckon that they deserve a hefty slice of Black Bun to restore some of their energy.

Communities in rural Scotland (and probably urban Scotland as well) are full of groups ceaselessly raising money for everything from the local playgroup to national charities and for a million other things besides. Fund-raising for these causes invariably includes coffee mornings or sales of work, and the star attraction at such events is the home-baking stall. Such stalls have to be seen to be believed, with tables laden with examples of this most traditional of Scots cooking, and from the moment the sale starts it usually takes about five or ten minutes to clear the baking tables completely. Such is the generosity of the Scots that they will bake tirelessly for these events and then spend liberally buying other people's works of culinary art.

Scotland abounds with small places advertising home baking, but the place I know best and have known since I was sixteen is the Laigh Bakehouse, in Hanover Street, Edinburgh. The Laigh was started by Moultrie Kelsall, the well-known Scots actor, who felt that Edinburgh needed a proper coffee-house, and he started the Laigh for his writing friends and his friends from the BBC as well as for Edinburgh people generally. The Laigh was officially opened by Sir Compton MacKenzie on 25 August 1958. When I was sixteen, and made my first acquaintance with the Laigh whilst a pupil at the crammers Basil Paterson's, my passion for the chocolate and coffee cakes was just greater than my terror of Moultrie Kelsall. He would prowl around, and I tried hard never to meet his eye – he was a most intimidating person. On the other hand, he did have the best cakes, short*cake* (as opposed to short*bread* which has a denser texture), coffee and lemon juice, and at lunchtimes wonderful soup and salads. All this could be enjoyed either in the company of friends or, if alone, with

Nineteenth-century silver tea-ware
from a collection at Ardsheal House.

Previous pages: The road bridge across the Beauly Firth, Inverness. Above: Looking up towards Edinburgh castle.

newspapers from the rack to peruse in peace as you ate. And woe betide you if you failed to fold the newspaper and replace it in the rack provided!

As a general rule, things one remembers fondly from long ago seem to be less good than they used to be. The one shining exception to this rule is the Laigh and the quality of the cakes and so on to be found there. The Laigh Bakehouse is now in premises further down Hanover Street from where it originally was, but still in a basement, and right next door to the Laigh kitchen, where all the baking is done and from where you can buy the produce to take home.

The Laigh is now owned and run by Joan Spicer. Joan, an elegant, effervescent woman, trained in Institutional Management and High Class Cookery at Atholl

Crescent, the renowned Edinburgh College of Domestic Science and Home Economy, now sadly defunct. Joan joined the Laigh as a baker, intending to stay only for a few months before moving to a job she had lined up in Chicago. But she never went to Chicago – the Laigh rapidly became, as she puts it, the love of her life, and she stayed on. She did leave once, just after she married, but she went back after two months to ask Moultrie Kelsall for part-time work. He replied, 'Darling, of course. Would 45 hours a week suit you?'

Joan is most ably supported by her husband in what is more a way of life than a job. She says she loves the countryside and would very much like to leave the city and go and live in the country, but she feels a responsibility to carry on what Moultrie Kelsall started. She was never frightened of Moultrie, whom she describes as the biggest influence in her life. It was Joan who made up the coffee cake recipe, and Joan who introduced the Hazelnut Meringue Cake into the Laigh repertoire.

For myself, I can never decide which I prefer, the Laigh chocolate or coffee cake. Both are sliced in oblong slices, with thick buttercream in the middle, and they are every bit as good now, in my forty-first year, when I shouldn't be indulging in such things, as they were in my sixteenth year, when I first tried them. Both the chocolate and the coffee cake are regularly dispatched in the diplomatic bag to Moscow and to Ankara. And as for the wonderful shortcake, crisp and crumbly and melt-in-the-mouth, way back in the 1960s an elderly lady ordered some six dozen and requested that they be carefully wrapped and packed, as she was taking them to the Kennedy family at Hyannisport. Since then several more consignments have followed.

The Laigh customers are a difficult lot. I should know, as I am a typical example. We like to find things unchanged, exactly as they always have been. There is a complaints book, and whenever Joan tries to introduce some new feature, at the expense of an old one, the complaints come flooding in. The public have blackmailed Joan into providing what they want – which is more of the same. There is something comforting about finding not only the chocolate and coffee cakes and the shortcake, but also the empire biscuits (echoes from the

Looking down from Calton Hill by the observatory onto Edinburgh's splendid Princes Street.

nursery), those white-iced, jam-filled biscuits, and the cheese scones, the hazelnut meringue and the chocolate fudge slices, just as there have always been. There is now carrot cake, too, and one or two other innovations which Joan has managed to slip in and get accepted by her fussy and particular clientele. The Laigh is a link with the past for so many of us, but it would never have been this way if the food hadn't been so good in the first place! The Laigh has been described as a 'lovely anachronism' – a most perfect description.

Joan loves her work and gets tremendous job satisfaction, never more so than during the three weeks of the Edinburgh Festival, when she gets to work at 5.30 a.m. instead of her usual 7.00 a.m. start. Her first customers are invariably the Breakfast Bunch, as they are known. They consist of a group of people who meet each morning in the Laigh, sitting always at the centre table, and who start their day with cheese scones and coffee, sometimes with champagne too. If for any reason one can't come, notes are left for the absentee in the table drawer, to be collected when convenient. Each Saturday morning throughout the year the atmosphere in the Laigh is that of a family party, with customers who have become friends and who meet up each week regularly on Saturday mornings. The Laigh is very much an Edinburgh institution, if not an institution in Scotland. And long may it go on, providing the very best examples of baking in Scotland in a totally unique atmosphere.

A posse of delivery bikes which seem to belong to the nineteenth-century.

APPLE PANCAKES WITH CINNAMON BUTTER

A pancake in Scotland is known as a drop scone in England (or a griddle cake in the US). This is a variation of mine on the more usual plain pancake batter. The cinnamon butter complements the apples in the pancakes beautifully.

Makes pancakes for 6 to 8 people

8oz / 1⅔ cups / 225g plain (all-purpose) flour
1 tbsp baking powder
2oz / ¼ cup / 60g caster (US granulated) sugar
½ tsp ground cinnamon
2oz / 4 tbsp / 60g butter, melted
2 size 1 or 2 / US extra large eggs, beaten
½ pint / 1¼ cups / 300ml milk
2 dessert apples – not Golden Delicious, which aren't delicious – peeled and cored
sunflower or other mild oil for frying

Cinnamon butter

4oz / 1 stick / 120g butter, softened
2 tsp ground cinnamon
4oz / ¾ cup / 120g light soft brown sugar

First make the cinnamon butter. Beat all the ingredients together until the mixture is smooth. Store in a covered container in the refrigerator until serving. (This keeps for 7–10 days.)

Sift the flour, baking powder, sugar and cinnamon into a bowl. Beat in the melted butter, beaten eggs and milk. Grate the apples into the mixture and mix in well.

Oil a griddle, or a heavy-based frying pan, or an electric hotplate, or if you have an Aga or Rayburn, the cooler hotplate. (For my American readers an Aga is a constantly burning range-like cooker with two or four ovens and hotplates. It gives an even heat and very consistent results.) Drop spoonsful of the apple batter on to the oiled surface, making pancakes of 2–3 inches / 5–7·5cm in diameter and leaving

Opposite: At Pittodrie, a welcoming fire greets you at tea time.
Above: A silver grape cutter.

a space between them. Cook for about 2 minutes or until small bubbles appear over the surface, then, with a palette knife (pancake turner), slip each over to cook on the other side.

As they cook, remove the pancakes and keep them warm on a plate, and covered with a cloth. When all the pancakes are cooked, serve them hot with the cinnamon butter.

BUNTY CREAMS

This recipe comes from Annette Stephen. She lives with us here, and does all the baking for the guests' teas. These are my most favourite of all the good things she makes. This recipe will give 11–12 finished biscuits (cookies) once they are sandwiched together with vanilla buttercream. If you prefer a plainer biscuit (cookie), just leave them single, without the buttercream.

Makes 22–24

8oz / 2 sticks / 225g butter
4oz / ½ cup / 120g caster (US granulated) sugar
2 tsp golden syrup (light corn) syrup
8oz / 1⅔ cups / 225g plain (all-purpose) flour
4oz / ½ cup / 120g cornflakes
2 tsp baking powder
1 tsp bicarbonate of soda (baking soda)
½ tsp vanilla essence (extract)

Buttercream (optional)

3oz / 6 tbsp / 90g butter, softened
3oz / ¾ cup / 90g icing (confectioners') sugar
vanilla essence (extract)

Beat the butter until softened, then gradually add the sugar and syrup and beat until well creamed. Mix in the dry ingredients and the vanilla. Roll into balls and arrange on baking sheets. Bake in a preheated oven (300°F / 150°C / gas 2) for 10–12 minutes, until they are golden brown. When you take them out of the oven, let them sit on the baking sheets for a minute, then carefully lift them off to finish cooling on wire racks.

Sandwich them together, if you like, with buttercream, made by beating the butter well with the sifted sugar and a few drops of vanilla.

TRADITIONAL SHORTBREAD

Of all Scottish food, perhaps shortbread is the best known.

Fills a baking tray about 10 x 12 inches/25 x 30cm.

1¼lb / 4 cups / 570g plain (all-purpose) flour
6oz / 1½ cups / 175g cornflour (cornstarch)
6oz / 1 cup / 175g caster (US granulated) sugar
1lb / 4 sticks / 450g butter
extra caster (US granulated) sugar, to dredge.

Sift the flour, cornflour and sugar into a mixing bowl. Cut the butter into the dry ingredients, then rub the butter in with your fingertips. Mix together well. You can also do this in a food processor, or in a tabletop food mixer.

Press the shortbread mixture into the tin. Prick the shortbread at even intervals with a fork, and bake in a preheated low oven (150°C / 300°F / gas 2) for about 1 hour, till the shortbread is a pale golden colour.

Take the tin out of the oven and dust the shortbread liberally with sugar, shaking it evenly over the surface. The sugar will stick to the hot shortbread. Cut the shortbread into squares or rectangle shapes, and cool on a wire rack. Store in an airtight tin.

CHOCOLATE TOFFEE SHORTBREAD

These are delectable for those with a sweet tooth and are also known as millionaire's shortbread.

Makes 12–16

Shortbread

6oz / 1½ sticks / 175g butter
6oz / ¾ cup / 175g caster (US granulated) sugar
8oz / 1⅔ cups / 225g plain (all-purpose) flour
2oz / ½ cup / 60g cornflour (cornstarch)
1 tsp baking powder

To make the shortbread layer, cream together the butter and sugar, beating very well. Sift together the flour, cornflour and baking powder and beat into the butter and sugar. Spread the mixture in a 12 inch / 30cm long baking tin, about 1–2 inches / 4–5cm deep and smooth even. Bake in a preheated moderate oven (350°F / 180°C / gas 4) for 20 minutes or until the shortbread is golden brown. Take the tin out of the oven and set aside to cool for 10 minutes while you make the caramel.

Fred and Gunn Erikson's glassware at Altnaharrie Inn.

Caramel

6oz / ¾ cup / 175g caster (US granulated) sugar
6oz / 1½ sticks / 175g butter
1 15oz / 450g can condensed milk
1 tbsp syrup
few drops of vanilla essence (extract)

To finish

6oz / 6 squares / 175g dark plain (semisweet) chocolate

Put all the ingredients for the caramel except the vanilla into a saucepan. Over a moderate heat, stir until the butter has melted and the sugar dissolved completely. Then bring the mixture to the boil and boil for 5–7 minutes. Take the pan off the heat, stir in the vanilla and continue stirring for 2–3 minutes to cool it slightly. Then pour it over the shortbread. Leave to cool completely.

To finish, melt the chocolate over hot water (take care not to overheat the chocolate) and pour it over the caramel layer. When it is cool, mark into squares with a sharp knife. Store in an airtight container.

BRAMBLE MUFFINS

I make these muffins when the brambles (what we call blackberries in Scotland) are in season, but they are very good made with other fruit too, such as blackcurrants or raspberries. The recipe was given to me by a friend in North Carolina and is for American-style muffins not the traditional British ones.

Makes about 24

12oz / 2½ cups / 350g plain (all-purpose) flour
6oz / ¾ cup / 175g caster (US granulated) sugar
2 tsp baking powder
½ tsp salt
2 size 2 / US extra large eggs
2oz / 4 tbsp / 60g butter, melted
½ pint / 1¼ cups / 300ml milk
8oz / about 2 cups / 225g brambles (blackberries) or other berries

Sift together the dry ingredients. Beat together the eggs, milk and melted butter. Stir into the dry ingredients and fold in the brambles. Line individual cake tins or deep bun tins (muffin tins) with paper cake cases and spoon the mixture into each, to come three-quarters up the sides.

Bake in a preheated moderate oven, (350°F / 180°C / gas 4) for 30–35 minutes. Leave a minute or two before serving, hot, with butter.

HAZELNUT MERINGUE WITH CHOCOLATE SAUCE

This recipe satisfies all that I love in a pudding – hazelnut meringue is one of my most favourite things, and so is a good dark chocolate sauce. The two together make for perfection as far as I'm concerned. Any leftover sauce keeps well in a screw-topped jar in the refrigerator.

Serves 8

Meringue

4oz / 1⅓ cups / 120g ground hazelnuts
4 size 2 / US extra large egg whites
8oz / 1 cup / 225g caster (superfine) sugar
1 tsp white wine vinegar
1 tsp vanilla essence (extract)

Chocolate sauce

½ pint / 1¼ cups / 300ml water
8oz / 1½ cups / 225g brown sugar
4 tbsp cocoa powder
1oz / 2 tbsp / 30g butter
1½ tsp vanilla essence (extract)
3 tbsp golden (light corn) syrup

To finish

¾ pint / 2 cups / 450ml double (heavy) cream, whipped
1 tbsp icing (confectioners') sugar
1 tsp cocoa powder

To make the meringue, first toast the hazelnuts: put them in a dry saucepan over heat, shaking the pan so as to brown the ground nuts evenly. (I seem able to burn batch after batch of nuts if I try to brown them in the oven or under a grill (broiler)! Set the nuts aside to cool.

Line the base of two 9 inch / 23cm sandwich cake tins (layer cake pans) with baking parchment and brush the sides with oil. In a bowl, whisk the egg whites until they are very stiff, then whisk in the sugar a spoonful at a time and continue whisking until the meringue is stiff. With a large metal spoon, fold the cooled toasted hazelnuts, the vinegar and vanilla quickly through the meringue.

Divide the mixture between the two prepared tins and smooth even. Bake in a preheated moderate oven (350°F / 180°C / gas 4) for 35 minutes. Take meringues out to finish cooling on wire racks.

To make the chocolate sauce, put all the sauce ingredients into a saucepan. Over a moderate heat, stir the ingredients until the sugar is dissolved, then let the sauce boil fast for about 5 minutes. The longer the sauce boils, the thicker it becomes.

To serve, put one meringue on a serving plate and cover it with the whipped cream. Put the remaining meringue on top, and dust the surface with the icing (confectioners') sugar mixed with the cocoa powder. Serve with the chocolate sauce.

*An elegant silver soup tureen
from the service at Inverlochy Castle.*

GINGER CARROT CAKE SQUARES

I can't imagine why I didn't think of adding ginger to my carrot cake recipe years ago,

it is so delicious. In all the variations on carrot cake recipes I still think this one, the one I've used now for 14 years, is the best. I bless the kind friend, Caroline Williams, who gave it to me all those years ago.

Makes 15–20 squares

½ pint / 1¼ cups / 300ml sunflower oil
10oz / 1¼ cups / 300g caster (US granulated) sugar
3 size 2 / US extra large eggs
6oz / 1¼ cups / 175g plain (all-purpose) flour
2 rounded tsp ground ginger
1 tsp bicarbonate of soda (baking soda)
1 tsp baking powder
1 rounded tsp ground cinnamon
½ tsp salt
8oz / 2 cups / 225g carrots, peeled and grated

Icing

6oz / 1½ sticks / 175g butter
6oz / ¾ cup / 175g cream cheese
8oz / 2 cups / 225g icing (confectioners') sugar
½ tsp vanilla essence (extract)
6 pieces of preserved ginger, cut into very fine slivers, to decorate

Line a 12–14 inch / 30–35cm long baking tin, about 2 inches / 5cm deep, with baking parchment. Put the sunflower oil into a large bowl and gently stir in the sugar. Whisk in the eggs, one by one, whisking well in between adding each. Sift in the dry ingredients and stir in the grated carrots, mixing all together well. Pour into the prepared tin. Bake in a preheated moderate oven (350°F / 180°C / gas 4) for 30–35 minutes. Take out of the oven and let the cake cool in the tin.

To make the icing, beat the butter and cream cheese until softened, then beat in the sifted sugar and vanilla.

When the cake is quite cold, spread the butter icing over the surface and scatter the slivers of ginger over. Cut the cake into squares. Store in an airtight container. This cake tastes better if it is eaten a couple of days after making rather than the same day.

THE SCOTTISH CHEESE BOARD

Until the last twenty years cheese was a pretty dismal subject in Scotland. There was Ayrshire Dunlop, a Cheddar type of cheese, and that was about it, apart from imported cheeses, and crowdie, a curd cheese, made domestically in the Highlands and Islands. But the last couple of decades have seen the Scottish cheese scene change dramatically, and there is now a wide range of delicious cheeses, made by enterprising individuals, from cow's, sheep and goat's milks.

Opposite: Rosemary Brocklehurst's goats at Lumsden, Aberdeenshire.
Above: A selection of soft and pressed goat's cheeses.

IN SCOTLAND, by law, all milk sold has to be pasteurized, whereas in England it is still permitted to sell unpasteurized milk, which is a totally different drink. This is one of the examples of the discrepancies that exist between Scottish and English law. However, the law does not apply to cheesemaking, and most of the really excellent cheeses on the market throughout Scotland are made from unpasteurized milk.

Here at Kinloch we have long since given up having a cheeseboard as such for our guests, with an assortment of about ten cheeses to choose from. We stopped because there was such a tremendous amount of wastage. Instead, we have a choice of three whole cheeses, and we treat cheese as a separate course, with the cheeses set out on the sideboard together with biscuits, oatcakes, celery and a big bowl of fruit, so that guests can choose whatever they like to eat with their cheese. By helping themselves, our guests can have as much or as little cheese as they want, and they can either have it following their pudding, or, as more and more people prefer these days, before the pudding. Personally, this is when I like to eat cheese.

The cheeses we have vary, but there is always a Stilton, made from unpasteurized milk, and a wax-wrapped Cheddar, usually a Curworthy, from Oke-hampton in Devon, which is made to a seventeenth-century recipe; because it is wax-wrapped the cheese is creamier and doesn't develop the sharp bite that cloth-wrapped Cheddars tend to take on as they age and dry. Our third cheese is either an Isle de France, or a St Aubrey. You will notice that we don't use Scottish cheeses on our menu; this is a calculated decision, taken because most of the other hotels mentioned in this book do have Scottish cheeses, and we feel that guests might feel like a contrast on arriving at Kinloch. Having said that, we ourselves are great cheese eaters, and we enjoy sampling Scottish cheeses with our family.

Above: These Dryfesdale cheeses are made from creamy cow's milk without any preservatives.
Opposite: Rolling countryside, Strathspey.

We have been very fortunate over the last two years in having a really excellent cheese specialist to supply us. Until two years ago we had the greatest difficulty getting cheeses of a consistently high standard. Then, at one of Irvine Robertson Wines' great tasting lunches, we were introduced to Trevor Knowles, of Moffat, Dumfries-shire. Trevor had provided the cheeses for the lunch. There began a very happy relationship between Trevor and Kinloch, which lasted until his recent and, for us, regrettable retirement. We had the distinction of being Trevor's first hotel customers, and he became our sole supplier of cheese. Trevor's interest in cheese was fired by Patrick Rance, the greatest expert on the subject in the world, and Trevor's knowledge and appreciation of cheese was soon almost equally impressive.

Keeping cheese is only a problem when the weather is hot. The quality of cheese doesn't improve if it is refrigerated, and we are lucky here in having a cool wine cellar, which is where we keep our cheeses. When the weather is exceptionally warm – and it can be, even in Skye – our cheeses have to go into the fridge. We cover them loosely with grease-proof paper, and make sure they emerge from the fridge about two hours before dinner is served. If they are wrapped in polythene they sweat. For the Stilton, we have an old china dish with a domed lid – the Stilton never goes into the fridge. There is dispute as to how to eat a Stilton – whether it should be sliced or dug into. Personally, I prefer to dig, and we have an antique Stilton scoop with a bone handle and a silver spoon, a gift from one of our guests. The reason why I prefer to use this scoop isn't just sentimental: digging is also practical, because it leaves us with the Stilton shell, and inevitably a fair amount of cheese is left inside the crust, which we use up in a variety of recipes. Stilton makes the most wonderful soup, but I always include apples or pears in the recipe, as well as celery; somehow the sweetness of

Goat's milk cheeses are still considered outlandish in Scotland but their popularity is growing as people come to appreciate their delicate flavour.

the fruit counteracts any sharpness of the Stilton. I also use Stilton in a choux pastry recipe, where the small balls of cheesy choux pastry are deep fried. They puff out as they fry, and turn a deep golden colour.

Fortunately there are very few people who can't eat cheese. In fact I can think of only one person in my acquaintance who can't touch any dish containing cheese. We make a number of dishes, usually as first course, with cheese as an ingredient. Among my favourites are Three Cheese Tart, with a tomato sauce as an accompaniment. Another great favourite is Herb Crêpes with a goat's cheese stuffing and which can be served either with a leek and nutmeg purée or with tomato sauce. One of our favourite supper dishes when the hotel is closed in winter is a cheese and garlic soufflé, which I make with a combination of Cheddar and goat's cheese.

The oldest type of cheese made in Scotland is crowdie. A curd cheese, made from cow's milk, it has been made in the highlands and islands of Scotland since before the Vikings. Crowdie has always been made domestically, but in 1962 Reggie and Susannah Stone began to make it commercially, using unpasteurized milk from their herd of dairy shorthorns. Crowdie used to be made by putting the container of fresh milk beside the heat on the kitchen range, or in the sun, till the milk soured. The natural souring of the fresh (unpasteurized) milk gave crowdie its citric lemony taste. When the soured milk has formed curds, with the consistency of scrambled eggs, these were mashed, mixed with salt and double cream, and then hung in a muslin to allow the whey to drip away. Some old people say that the crowdie in the muslin was traditionally left to hang on rowan trees, but why this should be I don't know. The rowan tree is viewed in Scotland with respect, as people still maintain that it has magic, or supernatural powers. But quite what this has to do with dripping whey from crowdie I don't know!

Nowadays, the Stones buy in pasteurized milk from the Milk Marketing Board. Pasteurized milk doesn't sour – it goes bad, so to start off the crowdie-making process they add lactic acid to the milk, but then make the crowdie in just the same way as it has always been made, down the centuries. They add a quarter of an ounce of salt to each pound of curd, and five pounds of double cream to 28 pounds of curd. They get thirteen pounds of crowdie from ten gallons of milk. With salt, crowdie keeps for about two weeks, but it freezes beautifully. Several years ago the Stones were contacted by Aberdeen Royal Infirmary, who asked them to make crowdie without salt, and to send it to them for their patients on kidney dialysis, who have to be on a very restricted diet. They had analysed the crowdie and found it to have a naturally low salt content, and to be very low in potassium and magnesium. The Stones now dispatch half-pound packages of their crowdie to hospitals throughout the country.

The Stones' farm cheesery is at Tain, in Ross-shire, where they make several cheeses besides crowdie. One, Caboc, a rich double cream cheese rolled in toasted pinhead oatmeal, is made from a recipe which has been passed down from mother to daughter in Susannah Stone's family and which dates back to Mariota de L'Ile, the romantic daughter of the fifteenth-century Lord of the Isles – which must relate our family with the Stones. I must say, if one could choose one's relations, I would be proud to be part of the Stones' family! Apart from their Highland crowdie, which in Ross-shire used to be eaten with oatcakes before a *ceilidh* (pronounced caily), a communal concert with audience participation – because it was thought to limit the effects of prolonged whisky drinking! – the Stones make Gruth Dhu, a crowdie cheese covered in toasted pinhead oatmeal and crushed black peppercorns, and galic, a soft cheese mixed with chopped wild garlic leaves, which are supposed to have 'all-healing' properties!

A cheese of some years' standing is the delicious Bonchester, made by John Curtis near Kelso. He set out to make a Brie-type of cheese based on a Coulommiers, from his unpasteurized Jersey cow's milk. The resulting cheese is as good as the best Brie I have ever tasted, and consistently good. As with all unpasteurized milk, John Curtis's cow's milk is regularly tested; in fact there have been around three hundred tests in the last four years. With cheeses made from unpasteurized milk there is variation caused by differences in the milk between summer and winter milkings, even on some occasions between morning and evening milkings, and milkings from different pastures.

A new cheese to the consumer is Dryfesdale, which takes its name from a village near Lockerbie, in Dumfriesshire. Made by Kathleen Davidson from a recipe which originates from Auchencruive Agricultural College in Ayrshire, Dryfesdale is completely natural, containing

A selection of regional Scottish cheeses which would delight any connoisseur.

no preservative, and therefore has only about a two-week shelf life. It is a firm, creamy cow's milk cheese, made with milk from a Friesian herd, and comes in four-ounce drum shapes. It was 'launched' when Trevor Knowles supplied 168 Dryfesdale cheeses for the 1989 SBAAT lunch in Edinburgh. SBAAT stands for the Scottish Business Achievement Award Trust, whose instigator and present chairman is Sandy Irvine Robertson. The Trust holds a prestigious annual lunch in Edinburgh, where the two-fold purpose of the day is to present an award to an outstanding businessman (or rather business person, although there has yet to be an award to a woman!) and also to raise money for charity – a different charity each year. The guest of honour at the 1989 lunch was the patron of the SBAAT, the Princess Royal.

Another favourite Scottish cheese of mine is stichell,

The evening sunlight dramatically catches the contours of the undulating Fife landscape.

made by Brenda Leddie at Kelso. Stichell is made from Jersey milk, and its texture is slightly crumbly, not unlike that of Lancashire cheese. Stichell is made in three sizes: half kilo, one kilo, and two kilos.

A traditional Scottish Cheddar, sometimes known as Tobermory Cheddar, is made by Jeff Reid. It is a good, strong Cheddar, cloth-wrapped, and made in a forty-pound wheel. Another Cheddar, this one wax-coated, is being made in Kintyre. It is so new that I haven't yet tried it, but if we like it we intend to replace our Curworthy Cheddar with the Kintyre cheese.

Rosemary Brocklehurst, originally from Yorkshire, is making goat's milk cheese in Aberdeenshire. Its trade name is Robrock, and there are eleven Robrock cheeses, which include Robrock Vine, which is wrapped in vine leaves, Robrock Mousec, a goat's milk cheese dipped in red wine, Robrock Sage and Robrock Chives, and Bennachie, which is a black wax-coated cheese. The newest of the range is Labueh, a goat's cheese stored in olive oil.

Ewe's and goat's milk cheeses are still a bit of an anathema in Scotland, but they are fast gaining in popularity and achieving overdue recognition. One of the earliest cheeses to be made from ewe's milk is Lanark Blue, made by Humphrey Errington in Lanarkshire. Humphrey Errington has done a great deal for the reputation of cheese in Scotland with his Lanark Blue and his Dunsyre, a creamy cow's milk blue cheese, made from Ayrshire's milk.

These are just a few examples of the results of the exciting trend in cheesemaking in Scotland today. It is really encouraging, and I foresee the day when Scotland will be as renowned for its cheeses as France.

STILTON, CELERY AND PEAR SOUP

The sweetness of the pears in this soup counteracts the acidity of the Stilton. It's a recipe I am often asked for by appreciative guests!

Serves 8

2oz / 4 tbsp / 60g butter
2 onions, peeled and chopped
4 celery sticks, chopped
2 pears, chopped – skin, core and all
2 pints / 5 cups / 1·25 litres chicken stock
6oz / 1½ cups / 175g Stilton cheese, crumbled
freshly ground black pepper
pinch of grated nutmeg
2 tbsp finely chopped parsley

Melt the butter in a saucepan and add the chopped onions and celery. Cook for about 5 minutes, stirring occasionally, then add the chopped pears and the chicken stock. Simmer gently for 20 minutes.

Cool the soup then liquidize it, adding the crumbled Stilton. Sieve the liquidized soup – this is the only way to get rid of the stringy celery bits. Pour the sieved soup into a clean pan, and season to taste with pepper and nutmeg (no salt is needed). Reheat and, just before serving, stir the chopped parsley through the soup.

LEEK AND NUTMEG PUREE

This thick purée is superb with cheesey dishes, particularly the herb crêpes with goat's cheese stuffing.

Serves 8

2–3 tbsp sunflower or other mild oil
1oz / 2 tbsp / 30g butter
6 medium-sized leeks, trimmed and sliced
salt and freshly ground black pepper
4 tbsp single (light) cream
½ tsp freshly grated nutmeg

Heat the oil and butter in a frying pan. Add the leeks and nutmeg and cook, stirring occasionally, until the leeks are quite tender. Season to taste with salt and pepper. Liquidize the leeks, adding the cream and the nutmeg. If the blades of the liquidizer or food processor aren't quite as sharp as they might be, sieve the purée, to remove all fibres.

Reheat gently, in a bowl over a pan of simmering water, to serve in spoonfuls beside the crêpes.

HERB CREPES WITH GOAT'S CHEESE STUFFING

I allow two crêpes per person for a first course and serve with the tomato sauce.

Serves 8

2 size 2 / US extra large eggs
4oz / ¾ cup / 120g plain (all-purpose) flour
pinch of salt
freshly ground pepper
½ pint / 1¼ cups / 300ml milk
2 tbsp cold water
few chives, snipped
small handful of parsley
some fresh tarragon leaves
2 sprigs of fresh dillweed

Filling

1lb / 450g goat's cheese, rind removed
2 egg whites

Break the eggs into a liquidizer or food processor and add the flour, salt and pepper to taste. Whiz, gradually adding the milk and water. Add the snipped chives, which unless snipped just wrap themselves around the blades, and the other herbs and whiz until the herbs are fine. Pour the crêpe batter into a jug and leave to stand for half an hour.

To cook the crêpes, melt a small amount of butter, about ¼oz / 1½ tsp / 7g in a crêpe or omelette pan, and swirl it over the surface of the pan. Pour in just enough batter to cover the bottom of the pan, swirling the batter around so that the crêpe will be as thin as possible. Over a moderate heat, cook for about 30 seconds, then turn the crêpe over using a small palette knife or spatula and your fingers. As they are cooked, stack the crêpes with a piece of greaseproof (wax) paper between each, to prevent them sticking together.

For the filling, put the cheese into a food processor with the egg whites and whiz until smooth.

Put a generous teaspoonful of filling in the middle of each crêpe and fold into a fat rectangle. Put the stuffed crêpes into an oiled or buttered heatproof dish and brush them with melted butter. Bake in a preheated moderate oven (350°F / 180°C / gas 4) for 20 minutes.

STILTON BEIGNETS

I allow 4 to 6 beignets per person. Exactly how many depends on the size – I aim for beignets about the size of a walnut. It also depends on how rich a main course and dessert are to follow the beignets.

An ornate carved sideboard from the dining-room of Inverlochy Castle.

Serves 8

5oz / 1 cup / 150g plain (all-purpose) flour
1 tsp mustard powder
3½oz / 7 tbsp / 100g butter, cut in bits
7fl oz / 200ml cold water
3 size 2 / US extra large eggs, beaten
1 garlic clove, peeled and crushed (minced)
4oz / 1 cup / 120g Stilton cheese, crumbled
sunflower oil for deep frying

Sift together the flour and mustard powder on to a piece of greaseproof (wax) paper. Put the pieces of butter and the water into a saucepan over a moderate heat. When the butter melts in the water, let the water come to a full rolling boil, then whoosh in the flour and mustard and beat hard, off the heat now, with a wooden spoon. Beat until the mixture comes away from the sides of the pan, which doesn't take very long. Gradually add the eggs to the butter and flour mixture. Beat until the eggs are incorporated and the paste is glossy. Beat in the garlic and the Stilton, and continue beating until the cheese has melted.

Heat oil for deep frying. Drop a few teaspoonfuls of the paste into the oil (to make walnut-sized beignets) and fry until puffed and golden brown all over. Drain on kitchen paper and keep warm in a low oven until all the beignets are fried. Serve hot.

The elegant menu from Pittodrie House.

TOMATO SAUCE

This is such a wonderful sauce for serving with all cheesey dishes, especially the herb crêpes with goat's cheese stuffing, the soufflé and the three-cheese tart.

Makes about 1 pint / 600ml

3 tbsp olive oil
2 onions, peeled and chopped
1 celery stick, chopped
1 carrot, peeled and chopped
14oz / 400g can tomatoes
2 tbsp tomato paste
1 garlic clove, peeled and chopped
salt and freshly ground black pepper
pinch of sugar
good pinch of dried basil, or 1 tsp pesto, or 2 tbsp chopped fresh basil

Heat the oil in a saucepan and add the chopped onions, celery and carrot. Cook for about 5 minutes, then add the canned tomatoes, tomato paste and chopped garlic. Season to taste with salt and pepper and add the sugar and dried basil or pesto (if you are using fresh basil, add it when you liquidize the cooked sauce). Simmer for 20–25 minutes, then cool and liquidize. Sieve the liquidized sauce, to remove the little tomato pips. Reheat to serve.

Herb crêpes with goat's cheese stuffing and tomato sauce.

GARLIC, CHEDDAR AND GOAT'S CHEESE SOUFFLE

I always think a plain cheese soufflé lacks something. The combination of cheeses plus the garlic makes this soufflé satisfy all my requirements.

Serves 4

2oz / 4 tbsp / 60g butter
1 large garlic clove, peeled and very finely chopped
2oz / 7 tbsp / 60g plain (all-purpose) flour
1 tsp mustard powder
1 pint / $2\frac{1}{2}$ cups / 600ml milk
salt and freshly ground black pepper
freshly grated nutmeg
3oz / $\frac{3}{4}$ cup / 90g Cheddar cheese, grated
3oz / $\frac{3}{4}$ cup / 90g goat's cheese, crumbled
5 size 2 / US extra large eggs, separated

Melt the butter in a saucepan and add the chopped garlic and flour. Cook for a few minutes, then stir in the mustard powder and gradually add the milk, stirring all the time until the sauce boils. Season to taste with salt, pepper and nutmeg, and stir in the grated Cheddar and the crumbled goat's cheese. Beat the egg yolks well into the sauce, one by one. Let the sauce cool completely. About 45 minutes before cooking time, whisk the egg whites until very stiff. With a large metal spoon, fold them quickly and thoroughly through the sauce. Pour into a buttered 3 pint / 2 quart / 1·75 litre soufflé dish and cover the dish with clingfilm (plastic wrap). The soufflé mixture won't collapse, and this saves last-minute whisking.

When you are ready, bake the soufflé, having removed the clingfilm (plastic wrap), in a preheated hot oven (425°F / 220°C / gas 7) for 40 minutes. A further 5 minutes in the oven past the cooking time won't hurt the soufflé, but as soon as it is taken out of the oven it must be served immediately as cooling soufflés collapse within minutes!

The cheeseboard with traditional oatcakes at Polmaily House.

THREE CHEESE TART

This tart makes a delicious first course, but it really benefits from the complementary flavours of either the tomato sauce or the leek and nutmeg purée.

Serves 8 as a first course, 4–6 as a main course

shortcrust (basic pie) pastry to line dish

Filling

3oz / 90g cream cheese, such as Philadelphia
3oz / $\frac{3}{4}$ cup / 90g Cheddar cheese, grated
about 3oz / 90g Brie or Bonchester cheese, white rind cut off
1 size 2 / US extra large egg

3 size 2 / US extra large egg yolks
$\frac{1}{4}$ pint / $\frac{2}{3}$ cup / 150ml single (light) cream
1 garlic clove, peeled and chopped
2 tbsp chopped parsley
dash of Worcestershire sauce
salt and freshly ground black pepper

Roll out the pastry and use to line a 9 inch / 23cm flan or quiche dish. Put it in the refrigerator to chill for at least 30 minutes, then bake it in a preheated moderate oven (350°F / 180°C / gas 4) for 20–25 minutes, until the pastry is golden brown.

Meanwhile, put the three cheeses into a food processsor and whiz, gradually adding the whole egg, the egg yolks, cream, garlic, parsley and Worcestershire sauce. Season with a pinch of salt and pepper to taste.

Pour the filling into the baked pastry case and return to the oven to bake for about 25 minutes, or until when you touch the surface the filling feels firm.

Serve warm.

USEFUL ADDRESSES

The following companies mentioned in the book all offer mail-order services.

Andy Race Fish Merchant
15 Industrial Estate
Mallaig
Inverness-shire PH4 4PB

Telephone 0687 2626

Naturally produced sea-food, including smoked fish and salted fish.
Large quantities delivered by van.
Contact: Andy Race

Cairngorm Whisky Centre
Inverdruie
Aviemore
Inverness-shire PH22 1QU

Telephone 0479 810574

Specialist in malt whisky, and supplies all other Scottish whiskies as well.
Frank Clark runs whisky tastings.
Contact: Frank Clark

Duncan Fraser
Game Dealer and Fish Merchant
17 Queensgate
Inverness IV1 1DP

Telephone 0463 232744

Game, poultry, white fish, smoked fish and oily fish.

Highland Fine Cheeses Ltd
Knockbreck Tain
Ross-shire IV19 1LE

Telephone 0862 2034

A wide range of traditional soft Highland cheeses
Contact: Jamie Stone

Irvine Robertson Wines
10 + 11 North Leigh Sands
Leith
Edinburgh EH6 4ER

Telephone 031 553 3521

A comprehensive selection of wines from all over the world. Scotch Whisky. Cigars.
Contact: Sandy Irvine Robertson

Lawrie & Sons Ltd
8, Industrial Estate
Mallaig PH41 4QD

Telephone 0687 2102

Most smoked fish in season only.
Contact: George Lawrie

Macbeth Butchers
20 High Street
Forres
Moray
Inverness-shire IV36 0DB

Telephone 0309 72254 and
034389 265 (after hours)

Hampers, gift packs, beef, game, smoked products, black pudding,
haggis and cheese.
Contact: Michael Gibson

Rannoch Smokery
Kinloch Rannoch
By Pitlochry
Perthshire PH16 5QD

Telephone 08822 344

Smoked venison only
Contact: Leo and Sarah Barclay

Scotherbs
Waterybutts Grange by Errol
Perthshire PH2 7SZ

Telephone 08212 228

Fresh herbs, quality seeds and plants, herb-based condiments and conserves.
Cookery demonstrations using herbs by Sue Turner.
Contact: Stan Turner or Robert Wilson

The Scottish Gourmet
The Thistle Mill
Station Road
Biggar ML12 6LP

Telephone 0899 21001

A gourmet club offering a mail-order service for Scottish specialities including smoked products, beef, cheese, pies, cakes and whisky.

Strathaird Salmon Farms
21, Longman Drive
Inverness IV1 1SU

Telephone 0463 225959

Smoked Salmon only.
Contact: Robert Taylor

Summer Isles Foods
The Achiltibuie Smoke House
Ullapool
Ross-shire IV26 2YG

Telephone 085 482 353

Smoked fish, smoked meat, delicatessen, game and poultry.
Contact: Audrey Ross

Valvona & Crolla
19 Elm Row
Edinburgh EH7 4AA

Telephone 031 556 6066

A comprehensive range of Italian wines.
Philip Contini runs an Italian Wine Tasting club.
Contact: Philip or Victor Contini

Walkers Shortbread Ltd
Aberlour on Spey AB3 9PB

Telephone: 03405 555

Shortbread, oatcakes, cakes, biscuits and meringues.
Contact: James Walker

Scottish Tourist Board
23, Ravelston Terrace
Edinburgh EH4 3EV

Telephone 031 332 2433

HOTELS

Airds Hotel
Port Appin
Argyll
Argyllshire PA38 4DF

Telephone 063 173 236/211

Altnaharrie Inn
Ullapool
Ross-shire IV26 2SS

Telephone 085 483 230

Ardsheal House
Kentallen
Appin
Argyll
Argyllshire PA38 4BX

Telephone 063 174 227

Cringletie House Hotel
Peebles
Peeblesshire EH45 8PL

Telephone 072 13 233

*Many Scottish hotels provide an
excellent base for hunting*

LOCATING THE HOTELS

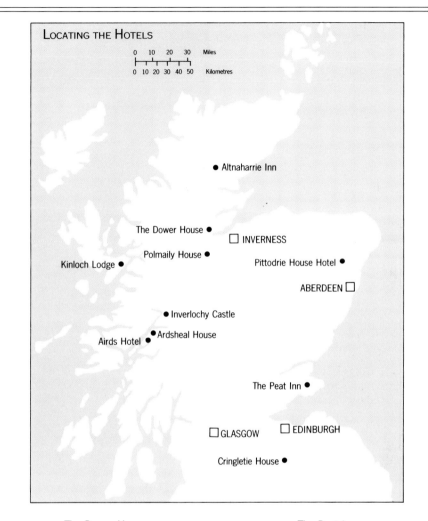

The Dower House
Highfield
Muir of Ord
Ross-shire IV6 7XN

Telephone 0463 870090

Inverlochy Castle
Fort William
Inverness-shire PH33 6SN

Telephone 0397 2177/2188

Kinloch Lodge
Sleat
Isle of Skye IV43 8QY

Telephone 04713 214

The Peat Inn
Peat Inn
Fife DY15 5LH

Telephone 033484 206

Pittodrie House Hotel
Pitcaple
Nr Inverurie
Aberdeenshire AB5 9HS

Telephone 04676 444

Polmaily House Hotel
Drumnadrochit
Inverness-shire IV3 6XT

Telephone 04562 343

Light Dishes and Starters

A selection of home-made sausages

Use the finest products to achieve the best results

Meat Dishes

Fish Dishes

The dining room at Polmaily House.

Looking through to the conservatory at Airds.